"A number of yea[rs] ... [st]arted out as a terrific worker, but [he] ... [he] became trapped in the compulsion to access it at the office instead of working. I had no idea how to help this man or handle his addiction, and at the time had no idea that this problem affects at least half the homes and businesses in the country. In *Porn@Work*, Michael Leahy bravely details his own history, demonstrates how this massive but unseen problem is destroying lives and careers, and provides an excellent road map for how to address it and bring healing."

Shaunti Feldhahn

Nationally syndicated newspaper columnist and bestselling author of
For Women Only: What You Need to Know About the Inner Lives of Men

---

"As a psychologist I have long worried about the impact of the Internet on culture. As CEO of a graduate school I am more aware than ever of the importance of preparing to deal with the sexualization of our culture. Michael Leahy has done all of corporate America a great service with this book."

C. Jeffrey Terrell, Ph.D.

President, Richmont Graduate University

"Porn addiction is a dirty little secret in the workplace. One of the reasons it is so difficult to stop porn in the workplace is that the very people with the authority are some of the same people with the problem... As a business consultant, I have seen the devastating effect of porn addiction on not only the people and families involved, but on the business and the employees."

Kevin Hanville

Business Consultant and National Speaker

"Shockingly honest! An eye-opening view of what's going on, how it happens, and what's really at stake. This book is for anyone who needs practical advice on how to protect their company from legal liabilities and help employees who may be caught in one of the most rapidly growing addictions of our time."

Patti Gordon
Speaker/Author of *Press Play*

"Porn in the office is today's 'elephant in the room.' Addictions to pornography have long been addressed at home. However, at work, the defenses of denial and rationalization are rampant. This has resulted in a shift in acting out from the home to the office... This book is an excellent starting place for anyone looking to address pornography in the work environment."

Glen Havens, M.D.
The Ark Psychiatric Services

"Revolutionary ... for cooperate America and the sexually addicted population. With a precise description of sexual addiction and its manifestations coupled with the lack of awareness in the workplace on such issues, Michael does a fantastic job of exposing the significant need for today's corporations. This book will jump start a new cultural phenomenon of healing individuals and making the workplace a safe place for help. The long-term effects of *Porn@Work* will increase productivity, lessen liability, cultivate community, and lay a solid foundation for the future workers, our children. Sexual addiction will not go away unless exposed, and with the information contained in these pages, the process has begun."

Troy Snyder, MS, NCC, LPC, CCSAS
Paraclete Counseling Center

"Shockingly real! I see the impact of pornography and sexual addiction on people's careers every day in my clients. Michael Leahy has done an outstanding job of showing the severity of the problem, its impact on employers and employees, and offering real solutions and hope to those who struggle with sexual addiction."

Richard Blankenship, LPC, NCC, CCSAS
Author of *S.A.R.A.H. (Spouses of Addicts Rebuilding and Healing)*,
L.I.F.E. Guide for Couples and *L.I.F.E. Guide for Young Men.*

"Michael Leahy knows first hand how destructive porn can be. Yet at the same time Michael knows there is hope. He honestly shares his own story so that the reader can get in touch with their story. In *Porn@Work* Michael offers hope for the struggling employee, counsel for the employer, and honest solutions to a very real problem that is affecting the workplace and the most valuable asset there— people. Michael highlights how porn erodes one's passion for real life and relationship, then offers a road back to the freedom and passion that porn depletes from good lives."

Marc V. Rutter
US National Director Leadership Development and Human Resources
Campus Crusade for Christ International

"Michael exposes a significant but rarely discussed issue that poses a real threat to businesses in today's culture. His personal experience plus facts and statistics make the book a compelling read but with practical solutions."

James L. Underwood
CPA/PFS, CFP®, Tarpley & Underwood, PC

PORN @ WORK

Exposing the Office's #1 Addiction

Michael Leahy

NORTHFIELD PUBLISHING

Chicago

© 2009 by
MICHAEL LEAHY

Published in association with the literary and editorial agencies of Credo Communications, Inc., 16778 S.E. Cohiba Ct., Damascus, OR 97089, www.sanfordci.com.

Cover design: DesignWorks Group
Cover photo: Shutterstock
Interior design: Smartt Guys design
Editors: Christopher Reese and Laura Lentz

Library of Congress Cataloging-in-Publication Data

Leahy, Michael, 1950-
   Porn@work : exposing the office's #1 addiction / Michael Leahy.
      p. cm.
   Includes bibliographical references.
   ISBN 978-0-8024-8129-0
   1. Pornography--Social aspects. 2. Computer sex. 3. Internet
addiction. 4. Work environment. I. Title. II. Title: Port at work.
   HQ471.L43 2009
   658.3'045--dc22

                              2009000958

We hope you enjoy this book from Northfield Publishing. Our goal is to provide high-quality, thought-provoking books and products that connect truth to your real needs and challenges. For more information on other books and products written and produced from a biblical perspective, go to www.moodypublishers.com or write to:

Northfield Publishing
820 N. LaSalle Boulevard
Chicago, IL 60610

1 3 5 7 9 10 8 6 4 2

Printed in the United States of America

*This book is dedicated
in loving memory of my father,*

RICHARD CHARLES LEAHY,

*A true champion of the American
free enterprise system*

Table of Contents

PREFACE

Still Addicted to Sex

As the Bill and Monica drama has shown, sex addiction is not necessarily what you thought it was. It is often not about the pervert, the exhibitionist, or the pornographer, although it can be. It is about your neighbor down the street who turns out to be, as everybody learns during the divorce, a hopeless woman-izer. It's about that sales associate with the slinky dresses and flirty smile who can't seem to behave herself when she's on the road. It's about the CEO and his "woman problem."[1]
—*Fortune*, May 1999

A decade ago, the headline blaring from the cover of *Fortune* magazine in May of 1999 read "Addicted to Sex: A Primal Problem Emerges from the Shadows in a New—and Dangerous—Corporate Environment." It was the first extensive article ever published by a prominent business magazine about the prevalence of pornographic sexual attitudes and sexual addiction within the business world, and the news was shocking. But for someone like me, a sex addict in recovery, it gave me a strange sense of hope. It meant that I was not alone in my day-to-day struggles with sex and porn at work.

Since then, the porn industry has mushroomed into a $97 billion a year global business, with $12 to14 billion spent in the U.S. alone.

Its largest distribution channel, of course, is the Internet, where access is as easy in the office cubicle as in the living room. While the use of porn at work is still a rather new and little-understood phenomenon, the impact it can have on shaping a person's sexual attitudes, beliefs, and workplace behaviors is unmistakable. I should know. My name is Michael Leahy and I'm a recovering sex addict. And my thirty-year relationship with pornography influenced every aspect of my life, including the choices I made at work and on the job while away from the office. You could say I'm intimately familiar with what *really* goes on behind closed doors and in the shadows of America's workplaces. It's a world that few people on the outside have ever seen and would probably never understand unless they spent a day in my shoes. Which is why I wrote this book.

Before I begin to share my "insider's" perspective on the pervasiveness of sex addiction and porn consumption at work, and strategies for dealing with it, let's look at a small sampling of some of today's sex scandal headlines, to see if much has changed since that day in 1999 when the rest of the world started to learn about what really goes on in the shadows of the office. While we don't know whether pornography played a role in every case of sexual misconduct cited, porn justifies and glamorizes such behavior—and the step from fantasizing to acting out on that fantasy is a short one.

INTERNET ADDICTION: THE NEXT DISABILITY?
—Human Resource Executive Online

The recent case of an IBM employee suing the company for wrongful termination after he was fired for using his work computer to visit an Internet sex-chat room may be a sign of things to come. . . .

James Pacenza is claiming protection under the ADA in his lawsuit against Armonk, N.Y.-based IBM for $5 million, saying he suffers from an addiction to pornography that was triggered by post-traumatic stress disorder arising from his service in the Vietnam War. . . .

Although the employee's argument that he suffers from an addiction to online pornography and is thus eligible for protection under the Americans with Disabilities Act may not stand up in court, others—including the authors of a recent university study—say that Internet addiction is indeed real. . . . Companies may find themselves liable for their employees' porn-related Web-surfing if they fail to take action.[2]

* * * *

EMPLOYERS HAVE DUTY TO INVESTIGATE WORKERS' ONLINE PORNOGRAPHY VIEWING
—Employment Law Information Network

In a decision that imposes broad obligations on employers, the New Jersey Appellate Division ruled last week that a company could be held liable for damages suffered by a victim of child pornography where it failed to investigate reports that an employee was viewing child pornography online while at work. The court held that an "employer who is on notice that one of its employees is using a workplace computer to access pornography, possibly child pornography, has a duty to investigate the employee's activities and to take prompt and effective action to stop the unauthorized activity." Finding that employees do not have privacy interests that would prohibit inspection of their workplace computers, the court held that an employer that fails to investigate information that an employee is viewing child pornography on the Internet while at work may be liable to a person subsequently victimized by the employee.[3]

* * * *

KNICKS LOSE BIG IN SEX HARASSMENT SUIT: COACH ISIAH THOMAS GUILTY; MADISON SQUARE GARDEN MUST PAY FORMER EXEC $11.6M
—CBS News

A federal jury decided Madison Square Garden and its chairman must pay $11.6 million in damages to former New York Knicks executive Anucha Browne Sanders in her sexual harassment lawsuit.

A verdict earlier Tuesday found that Knicks coach Isiah Thomas subjected Browne Sanders to unwanted advances and a barrage of verbal insults, but that he did not have to pay punitive damages.

The jury did find, however, that Madison Square Garden committed harassment against the woman and decided she was entitled to punitive damages. The Garden said it would appeal.[4]

* * * *

A SEX SCANDAL IS IN THE MIX AT SARA LEE
—Fortune

Sara Lee's CEO runs a public company, but this summer he's been embroiled in a scandal involving a very private matter. In late July, Brenda Jarvis, 35, filed a sexual-discrimination lawsuit against Sara Lee's chief executive, C. Steven McMillan, and the $20 billion packaged-goods company, alleging that the CEO had offered her a job, then rescinded after she declined to continue a sexual relationship.

McMillan's plight is unusual. While high-profile sex scandals do occur in corporate America, more often than not CEO dalliances don't make headlines, and legal matters are usually settled behind closed doors. In Sara Lee's case, the company balked at attempts to settle privately, according to Jarvis's lawyer, Martin Oberman. Instead Sara Lee, which owns several brands that cater to female consumers—Playtex, L'Eggs hosiery, and Wonderbra among them—now plans to defend McMillan in what's sure to be a nasty courtroom dust-up. A court date is set for Aug. 27.[5]

* * * *

FEDEX DRIVER WINS SEX-HARASSMENT CASE
—Human Resource Executive Online

A federal jury has returned a $3.2 million verdict in favor of a female truck driver who was subjected to sexual harassment and then became the target of intimidation after she challenged the harassment.

Marion Shaub, 47, was the only woman driver at the Federal Express Corp. facility (the company is a unit of Memphis, Tenn.-based

FedEx Corp.) at Harrisburg International Airport in Middletown, Pa., from 1997 to 2000.

During that period, according to her complaint, she was subjected to a steady stream of sexual innuendo and harassment by co-workers. Among other comments, Shaub testified she was told women should be "barefoot and pregnant" and that she "looked like a porn star." One male colleague told Shaub that if she were his daughter, "he would abort her."[6]

* * * *

INTERIOR DEPARTMENT OFFICIALS ALLEGEDLY HAD ILLICIT SEX WITH OIL COMPANY WORKERS
—San Jose Mercury News

Government officials handling billions of dollars in oil royalties improperly engaged in sex with employees of energy companies they were dealing with and received numerous gifts from them, federal investigators said Wednesday.

The alleged transgressions involve 13 former and current Interior Department employees in Denver and Washington. Their alleged improprieties include rigging contracts, working part-time as private oil consultants, and having sexual relationships with—and accepting golf and ski trips and dinners from—oil company employees, according to three reports released Wednesday by the Interior Department's inspector general.

The investigations reveal a "culture of substance abuse and promiscuity" by a small group of individuals "wholly lacking in acceptance of or adherence to government ethical standards," wrote Inspector General Earl E. Devaney. Devaney's office spent more than two years and $5.3 million on the investigations.[7]

* * * *

SPITZER IS LINKED TO PROSTITUTION RING
—New York Times

Gov. Eliot Spitzer, who gained national prominence relentlessly pursuing Wall Street wrongdoing, has been caught on a federal *wiretap arranging to meet with a high-priced prostitute at a Washington hotel last month, according to a law enforcement official and a person briefed on the investigation.[8]*

* * * *

DUCHOVNY IN REHAB
— New York Times

David Duchovny has entered a rehabilitation center for sex addiction, The Associated Press reported. Mr. Duchovny, who plays a sex-obsessed character on the Showtime show "Californication," did so voluntarily, according to a statement on Thursday from his lawyer, Stanton Stein. The statement also quoted Mr. Duchovny as saying, "I ask for respect and privacy for my wife and children as we deal with this situation as a family." Mr. Duchovny has been married to the actress Téa Leoni since 1997. They have two children. The second season of "Californication" begins on Sept. 28.[9]

* * * *

LORD LAIDLAW SEEKS HELP FOR SEX ADDICTION AFTER LURID REVELATIONS
— The London Herald

With his homes in Monaco, South Africa and the French Riveria, a yacht, his own vineyard and private jet, Irvine Laidlaw is used to the good life. The son of a mill owner, from Keith, near Aberdeen, the Tory peer spent years building up the world's largest conference organising business, which he sold three years ago for nearly £770m.

Until this weekend, the 65-year-old was perhaps best known for his philanthropy, funding inner city academies and youth projects for disadvantaged children in Scotland.

Yet yesterday, following a tabloid article featuring allegations of prostitutes, cocaine and a 22-year-old Vogue model, Lord Laidlaw of Rothiemay, Scotland's fourth-richest man, admitted he was being treated for sex addiction. . . . It's a condition he claimed he had been suffering from all his adult life.[10]

* * * *

REP. FOLEY QUITS IN PAGE SCANDAL
—The Washington Post

Six-term Rep. Mark Foley (R-Fla.) resigned yesterday amid reports that he had sent sexually explicit Internet messages to at least one underage male former page.

Foley, who was considered likely to win reelection this fall, said in a . . . letter of resignation: "I am deeply sorry and I apologize for letting down my family and the people of Florida I have had the privilege to represent."[11]

* * * *

TECHNOLOGY MAKES PORN EASIER TO ACCESS AT WORK
—USA Today Cover Story

More than a decade after employers began cracking down on those who view online pornography at work, porn is continuing to create tension in offices across the nation—in part because laptop computers, cell phones and other portable devices have made it easier for risk-takers to visit such websites undetected.[12]

INTRODUCTION

Every Office's Dirty Secret

If you've worked in an office at some point, you've probably been in this situation or one similar. You walk by a fellow employee's desk or cubicle and your eyes glance over their shoulder to see what they're doing. Whether your sneak peek is an innocent subconscious reflex, just idle curiosity, or an intentional act that you feel is necessary as a manager or supervisor, it's what you didn't expect to see on that computer screen that stops you in your tracks. Pornography. On a computer screen. At work.

- At $13.3 billion, the 2006 revenues of the sex and porn industry in the U.S. were bigger than the revenues of the NFL, NBA, and Major League Baseball combined.

- 70% of all online porn access occurs during the nine – five workday.

- Two-thirds of 474 human resources professionals said in a survey they've discovered pornography on employee computers. Nearly half of those, 43%, said they had found such material more than once.

While catching someone you know and work with every day in the act of ogling over porn is always startling, the secondary reactions and emotions vary widely. Some people are shocked and highly offended while others just brush it off. Some are hurt and angered by its very presence at work, while others seem amused or even mildly titillated by the whole thing. While it's a big deal to some, others may be mystified by all the fuss surrounding their co-workers' Web surfing preferences. "It's no big deal really," they reason. "After all, it's just porn."

Regardless of how one feels about it on a personal level, porn at work is a big deal and a serious workplace issue for both employees and employers. "Liability is the thing that keeps me up at night, because we are liable for things people do on our premises," says Richard Laermer, CEO of the public relations firm RLM. "It's serious. I'll see somebody doing it, and I'll peek over their shoulder, and they'll say, 'I don't know how that happened.' It's like 10 year olds. And it's always on company time."[1]

> **"The sex down on Wall Street is unbelievable, with the prostitution and the porn. It is huge."**
>
> Stephen Pesce, a New York City psychotherapist and interventionist, quoted by Betsy Morris, "Addicted to Sex," Fortune, May 10, 1999.

Laermer and other CEOs have good reason to be concerned. With 16% of men and 8% of women admitting to visiting porn sites while at work,[2] the heightened concerns over increased litigation risk due to sexual misconduct at work are very well founded. According to a survey conducted in 2005 by the American Management Association, about one in four companies have fired an employee for misusing the Internet. And the number of lawsuits brought against companies by the Equal Employment Opportunity Commission based on complaints by people who claimed they saw co-workers viewing or distributing adult-oriented material at work continues to rise, as does the number of other types of sexual harassment lawsuits.

Whether such situations generate mild tremors or trigger major shock waves in the organization, everyone is affected when a co-worker or leader is exposed and humiliated over their "sexual indiscretions." Spokespersons and PR firms try to spin these revelations in the best light possible in hopes of salvaging a career and the company's reputation. But careers and reputations seldom fully recover from such scandals, especially for those in the executive suite.

For the rest of us, hardworking men and women who give two-thirds of our waking hours during the week to our jobs and the companies who employ us, what happens to us when we fall, or when one of our co-workers or leaders betrays our trust? What about the organizations and office staff and strategic partners who were all once an integral part of that person's personal supply chain? Like the families and loved ones who trusted that person and supported them, everyone gets hurt in the end. The embarrassing fall from grace, no matter how big or how small, takes something away from all of us as we come to realize that our trust has been broken, either by something we did or by something done to us by others.

As we try to pick up the pieces and repair the damage in the wake of these sexual improprieties, we all have to ask ourselves "What's really going on here?" and "Why didn't anyone see it coming?" For those looking for answers, and the means and motivation to deal with these situations before they erupt, this book was written for you. The problem is complex, and I don't pretend to have all of the answers detailed, or even the problems thoroughly analyzed. But what I can give you is some straight talk and an insider's perspective on sex and pornography addiction that most people in the business world have never gotten. My vantage point is unique because I was that person who is every line manager's and HR professional's worst nightmare—the sex addict at work who flew under the radar for years and never got caught. The sexual harassment perpetrator or hostile workplace environment creator who slipped by without being noticed even though the signs were everywhere if only people at work had known what to look for. I was the headline that never happened, but I was also the sales star that never rose and the top performer that should have been.

I realize you may have picked up this book because it's part of your job to better understand emerging workplace issues like how and why employees risk their jobs and careers through their use of Internet pornography at work, or by exhibiting inappropriate or out-of-control sexual attitudes and behaviors on the job. Whether you are a human resources professional, a midlevel manager, or even a senior executive or business owner, you are responsible for managing people and maximizing their productivity to help your organization achieve its mission. Of course, that job description involves ensuring that potential costs and consequences are held to a minimum, especially as they relate to negatively impacting the bottom line or threatening the achievement of mission objectives. I want you to know that this book was written with you in mind and is based on the assumption that your knowledge about the subject matter is probably limited. Perhaps your only exposure to these issues has been trying to resolve past sexual misconduct incidents at work. My hope is that this book and my insights will provide you with a fresh, new perspective that you can use to more effectively recognize and respond to or even prevent such incidents in the future. I want to help you "get inside the head" of a typical employee who is struggling with sexual compulsivity and addiction at work so you will have a better understanding of what they're really thinking and why they're doing what they do.

If you are a health care professional or medical practitioner looking to stay current with the latest information in the field as it relates to the manifestation of sexual addiction in the workplace, I'm hoping that you, too, will benefit from my personal insights and experiences as well as those of others I have cited. For those of you who work with sex addicts and their families on a regular basis, much of what I share may be familiar to you. But what might be new is the focus of this book on how sexual addiction plays out in the work environment and informed strategies for dealing with it.

Finally, for that group of readers who make up the millions of men and women and their loved ones who are somewhere in the midst of this struggle I speak of, do not lose hope. If you've asked for help and have found a safe place to heal in counseling and/or in a recovery or support group, I implore you to continue moving courageously down the hard road of recovery. If you still consider yourself to be a recreational user of porn who is absolutely convinced he can manage his use of the material without suffering the consequences you'll read about here, I urge you to heed the warnings that follow. There's nothing more disheartening than an addict in denial. If you don't believe me, I dare you to really start listening to those around you whom you're hurting and who have tried to get you to stop. There is a spouse or parent or sibling or child who is dying inside and searching for any hope that you, the addict, will wake up one day and come back to them. Their words and this book may very well be the last voice of truth you ever hear as you continue down a path that will very likely destroy everything you hold dear. Because by the time you realize that it's no longer recreational, it's usually too late. So you need this book as much, if not more, than everyone else. You need it to help you wake up to the reality of where you are and where you're headed before you lose the ability to make that assessment on your own.

For those who are wondering what other qualifications I have to be speaking out so boldly on the subject of sex and porn at work, there are several. First, my story is typical of many men my age (I am fifty years old as I write this), who are in their prime earnings years and are at or approaching the apex of their careers in terms of position and responsibility, not to mention vulnerability.

After being exposed to pornography as an eleven-year-old, I spent the next thirty years of my life pursuing the material in its various and evolving forms. As I consumed pornography, I started to find my sexual identity and define my self-image in the pages of adult magazines. I started believing at a young age that to be a "real man" meant being sexual with a lot of women. As the youngest of five in a boomer generation family, I was an alert observer of the sexual revolution of the '60s and the normalization of porn in our culture and mainstream media throughout the '70s and '80s. When Internet porn debuted in the '90s, I was an able and willing early adopter of both the medium and the message. That's when my penchant for porn accelerated into a compulsive and destructive sexual addiction. My hidden life of sexual "acting out" behaviors escalated to the point of having an affair with a customer who was herself a love and relationship addict. A couple of years and many bad decisions later my fantasy world came crashing down.

Although I've been in recovery from sexual addiction for ten years now, the consequences of my actions cost me my fifteen-year marriage and family of two boys, countless family and friendship relationships, my reputation and standing in the community, a lot of money, and a promising business partnership with my brother's firm. The hard work of recovery has paid off—mainly, I believe, because I was eventually willing to see beyond the physiological, behavioral, and emotional issues related to my addiction and deal also with the relational and spiritual issues that were at the root of my problem. When I finally hit bottom and had no other choice but to acknowledge that I wasn't God, my life started to change from the inside out. I have since witnessed firsthand the reconciliation and restoration of many broken relationships, including my and my ex-wife's families, my boys, and my ex-wife and her husband (she remarried a couple of years after our divorce)—all of them miracles in my book. Today I am experiencing true freedom from my sexual addiction like I've never known before and healthy, vibrant relationships with others. In fact, after years spent struggling with honesty and openness in one relationship after another, I have since remarried and am living proof that even the most hopeless addict is capable of experiencing full recovery and making a successful comeback.

My second qualification for speaking out in this area relates to the fact that throughout my thirty-year relationship with pornography, the resulting pattern of secret, inappropriate sexual behaviors played itself out largely in the workplace. As a sales executive in the computer industry for over two decades, I worked for everyone from blue chip giants like IBM, NEC, and Unisys to midsized dot-coms and small-business start-ups like Open Text, Everex Systems, Optio Software, and Jamcracker. In other words, I've been an active participant at all levels in one of the biggest threats to businesses and heaviest drains on worker productivity in the history of the American free enterprise system. By today's legal standards, I put most companies I worked for at risk of experiencing costly sexual harassment or hostile workplace environment lawsuits—had I been caught. During that time I stole thousands of hours from my former employers, most of whom had hired me to generate millions of dollars in revenue each year in my respective sales territories. Because of my growing obsession with porn, I did just well enough to get by, most of the time. Other times I didn't and either quit, was let go in a reduction in force, or was out-and-out fired for poor performance. In any event, I've been there and I know all of the secrets and tricks that your sexually addicted employees are using to avoid getting caught.

After spending twenty years perfecting the art of hiding my growing addiction and deceiving my employers, I've since spent the past ten years of my recovery not only helping others overcome their sexual addictions, but also coaching and consulting individuals and business leaders on how to restore sexual integrity to their lives and businesses. In the process I've become an activist of sorts, having founded BraveHearts, an advocacy group that trains people who are experiencing freedom from sexual addiction to use the power of their personal story to inspire hope and bring freedom to others, including the victims. By using our stories to raise the public's awareness of the hidden dangers and long-term consequences of pornography consumption and the sexualization of our culture, we hope to see the realization of our vision—the restoration of sexual integrity to all of humanity. A priority toward that end is to raise up an army of voices to help curb the growing worldwide demand for the sex trafficking of millions of innocent women and children. In other words, I've not only returned to the business world as the founder and leader of a thriving small business, but I've also been successful at channeling my newfound passion to help others see a bold new vision for bringing about seismic change in sexual attitudes and social justice for victims of sexual abuse in our world.

The third qualification I bring to this discussion should be of great interest to managers, executives, and HR professionals. For the past four years, I've had the opportunity to give my "Porn Nation" live-speaker, multimedia-intensive presentation to over 100,000 college and university students on over 150 campuses throughout the world. My interactions with this present and future workforce have taught me a lot about the sexual attitudes and behaviors they'll be bringing with them to work upon graduation. In fact, we've even conducted the largest sex survey of its kind ever done on this demographic. Over 25,000 college students have told us what they really think and feel about pornography on campus, and how they actually interact with it. I'm anxious to share with you the key results of this massive, multi-year survey in this book. These will be important clues to the rest of us about what we might expect when these Millennials finally graduate and show up for work. (For a more in-depth analysis of the results of this sex survey and their implications, see my recent book *Porn University: What College Students Are Really Saying about Sex on Campus*.) The bottom line is *Porn@Work* is a book I believe we all must read sooner or later. Because one way or another, we are all affected by this sociosexual health epidemic sweeping the nation. As long as pornography is so easily accessible, especially for children and adolescents, we always will be. That's just the way pornography and its by-products, sex syndrome (which I will describe in chapter 5) and sexual addiction, work. In subtle and not-so-subtle ways, sexual images and messages have a way of interrupting the flow of our lives. Whether we are at home, work, or school, exposure to sexual images and messages will always affect us because we are by nature sexual beings. At the very least, our little surprises back at the office will certainly change the way we think of our unfortunate co-worker (or manager or CEO) offenders. And what if it's our spouse or significant other? Is it possible that our hypersensitive society is blowing the whole Internet porn in the office thing out of proportion, as many people claim? Or are we truly headed for a day of reckoning on an issue that few of us want to face or talk about but nearly everyone is somehow affected by?

How you answer those questions says a lot about how prepared you are to deal with the hidden sexual realities of the present and future workforce. While I've found that most people are naive when it comes to understanding sexual compulsivity and addiction—a condition that affects anywhere from sixteen to twenty-one million men and women in our country alone—there is even less awareness of how sex addicts and sex addicts-in-the-making operate at work and threaten the viability and effectiveness of our organizations. These are the issues I aim to clarify and discuss in the pages of this book.

To help you gain a better understanding of what sexual addiction at work really looks like and what we can do to help those affected by it in order to restore sexual integrity to the workplace, I've divided the book into three major sections.

In Part 1, Employees Behaving Badly, I share my story and personal experiences to bring you the reader into the hidden world of a sex addict at work. I'll talk about what that looked like for me and others as well as discuss the toll this exacts on co-workers, business associates, and families. I'll also unpack the key societal factors that are coming together to create a "perfect storm" that's helping to fuel this epidemic.

In Part 2, Why They Won't Stop, I explain why it's so hard (if not impossible) for those who struggle to stop on their own. We'll also take a closer look at why an addict thinks and feels the way they do in an office environment, as well as the telltale signs you should be looking for that might indicate an employee is addicted. Finally, we'll take a closer look at the sexual attitudes, beliefs, and behaviors of today's college students, the newest members of our workforce.

In Part 3, Finding A Better Way to Work, we'll begin by looking at what we might expect when the world of today's sexually desensitized college graduates collides with the much less sexually tolerant world of work. I'll also talk about every CEO's worst nightmare, business-crippling litigation due to sexual misconduct in the office, and what employers and managers can do today to lessen their risk of losing millions and suffering permanent damage to their business and their brand due to sexual harassment and hostile workplace environment lawsuits. I will close this section by offering a simple yet proven first step to solving this complex and growing workplace issue that any business can employ.

I conclude this book by personally challenging every CEO and business owner to join me in the fight to bring sexual integrity back into the workplace. The key is restoring respect for the individual as a core value and demonstrating that commitment by dealing with all employees equally, including those who are found to be struggling with sexual compulsivity and addiction but who want to get well.

For those who are sexually addicted or are a loved one of someone who is, I want you to know why I have targeted the first several books I've written on this topic to people other than you. Books on recovery and healing that I am eager to write will come soon. But it has been my long-held belief that by sharing our stories, and mine in particular, with others who may not understand or share in our struggles, that they will gain a better understanding of the chaotic battles that rage inside of us. I do this in the belief that as more people hear our stories and become aware of what sexual compulsivity and addiction is really all about, they will come alongside individuals like you and me to offer hope and help.

Finally, I am only one voice, but God willing many more will soon follow. I firmly believe that the time has come for all of us to work together in order to bring hope and help to the millions of people who want to get well. For employers to provide those who struggle with sexual addiction the same opportunities for healing that they readily extend to our fellow addicted co-workers who simply have a different drug of choice. And for those of us who have been redeemed, that we would also lend our voices to serve greater causes than our own and help turn back the terrible tide of global sex trafficking so that millions of oppressed women and children can be set free from the evils of sexual terrorism. To this end—freedom for the oppressed and sexual integrity restored to all of humanity—I have dedicated this book and the rest of my life. I hope after reading this book that you, too, will see fit to join us in this worthy cause.

Part 1

Employees
Behaving Badly

A PENCHANT *for* PORN

It has to rank as one of the lowest points of my career, if not my life— but strangely enough, I don't really remember how I felt at the time. Indifferent perhaps. Maybe I was just numb to it all. Not remembering perplexes me to this day. I mean, how does a person not remember how it felt to be fired from a job by your

- **Every second in the U.S., $3,075 is spent on pornography, 28,258 Internet users view pornography, and 372 Internet users type adult search terms into search engines.**

- **The largest consumer of Internet pornography is the 35–49 age group.**

own brother? While I may not be able to recollect exactly what I was feeling at that time, I do remember the circumstances surrounding this most embarrassing moment.

It was 1997, the year before my divorce. Earlier that year, I had started an affair with another woman. My wife suspected something was going on and I finally confessed it to her three months later. But in spite of truly feeling sorry for what I had done and promising to stop the affair, I continued seeing my affair partner in secret on and off for the next year and a half. In the process, everything else in my life took a backseat to this self-destructive, illicit relationship I was involved in—my marriage, my two boys, my job, my friends, and family. At the drop of a hat, or the ring of my cell phone, or the vibration of my pager, I would stop everything and leave what I was doing just to be with her. Long after I left my wife and family, I finally came to realize I had lost everything, literally.

Her name was Teresa and she was actually a customer of mine whom I had met at work. Several years before, I had left my fifteen-year career in the computer industry to take a break and do something low tech and less stressful for a change. I was starting to get burned out by the breakneck pace of being a business-to-business sales executive in the computer industry, something I'd been doing ever since I went to work for IBM straight out of college. But there was more to it than that. I had grown dissatisfied with my admittedly comfortable standard of living and was looking for a way to get off the corporate treadmill, make more money, and become financially independent. In other words, I was greedy and wanted more. I had always been intrigued by my brother's successful, rapidly growing business and was convinced that there was a big market in my hometown of Atlanta for their custom wine cellars, saunas, and steam rooms. So after kicking around the idea for a couple of years, my brother and his partner finally agreed to let me open up their first branch office beyond their home base of Seattle, Washington.

By the time I met Teresa, I had the business rolling along pretty well. I had grown it from a one-man show to having several employees. We all worked out of a small, refurbished warehouse space located in the far suburbs of Atlanta close to where I lived. It was complete with shop space and offices and a product showroom we used for potential customers. Although it was a far cry from my offices at IBM, NEC, or Unisys, it was something I could say I started and built up myself. The prize in all of this hard work was a potential stake in the larger business that my brother and his partner had worked hard for many years to build. My job was to serve as the Atlanta branch manager, but with fifteen plus years of sales experience, I always dabbled in the sales side of things and kept in close contact with our customers. So when the call came in that a woman was interested in spending well into five figures with us (our definition of a major client), I naturally wanted to be involved.

Meeting people and making new friends came easily to me. But from the very first phone conversation I had with this prospective client, I could tell there was more in the offing here than just a big sale. We flirted back and forth with each other during the "tell me about yourself" phase of our initial phone conversations. She was shopping for a steam room and a wine cellar to outfit a new home her fiancé was building, but she didn't talk like a woman in love. I had been married for thirteen years, but had been slowly convincing myself over the past several of those that I somehow deserved a better life than the one I was living—in spite of having a devoted wife and a loving family who stood by my side through all of my ups and downs. At that point, I was an affair waiting to happen.

I had grown increasingly impatient with my lot in life in those days and was envious of and lusting for everything everyone else had that I didn't—bigger homes, better jobs, newer cars, younger wives, you name it. I was having a classic midlife crisis and nothing seemed to satisfy me anymore. I had taken a big cut in pay to join my brother's business right after one of my best years ever in sales in the computer industry. I had a great job and a lot of money in the bank. Nonetheless, I convinced my wife and kids that we needed— no, deserved—much more. We deserved to live in a better neighborhood and a bigger house, where I believed we'd make better friends and be so much happier than we were then. So I convinced us to leave our good and faithful friends behind and moved out of our affordable and more than adequate home into an upscale, country club-style neighborhood full of people we didn't know and a new 5,000-square-foot home that we really couldn't keep up with, much less afford.

I had also decided my present job in the computer industry wasn't going to be enough to get us to the new and improved promised land of our upscale American dream. So after that best year ever in sales, I quit as soon as I could strike a deal with my brother and his partner. The golden egg was the promise of an ownership stake in the business, if things should work out. Of course, expanding a small business on limited resources takes extra time and a lot of hard work and luck along the way. The business was growing, but not fast enough for my liking. And not fast enough for me to avoid maxing out our credit cards and dipping into our 401K retirement savings regularly to help make ends meet. Instead of growing richer and settling comfortably into our new lifestyle, we were growing poorer by the day and sinking further into debt. I tried to hide my discontent from my wife and kids by working longer hours and stuffing my feelings of frustration and anxiety while I was around them. But over time that only made the distance that was starting to grow between us seem larger and harder to bridge. I could feel my new and improved version of the American Dream slipping away.

But when Teresa pulled up to our less than glamorous office/warehouse for the first time, no one there, including me, was thinking much about anything or anyone else but her. As she brought her candy apple red, late model Mercedes 500SL convertible to a stop in our parking lot, the car door opened and out stepped a tall, tanned, blonde bombshell of a woman wearing sunglasses and a glamorous summer dress. The guys in the office and those out in the shop froze and gawked at her right up until she came through the front door, at which point they suddenly pretended to look busy and otherwise preoccupied. To them, this was a pleasant surprise and a refreshing break in what had been a brutally hot and humid workday. To me, I suddenly saw more than just another pretty woman and the possible beginnings of a sexual fling. I saw a potential meal ticket—a permanent solution to all of my problems. I knew her car alone was worth more than I made in two years' time and I wondered if there was more where that came from.

The flirting continued in my office that day, in follow-up phone conversations, and on the private plane ride to and from Alabama several days later to take measurements at the fiancé's new construction home. Finally, all the playful talk and mild advances gave way to our first sexual encounter. She was ready to sign a sales contract, so we agreed to meet at her apartment in Atlanta's ritzy Buckhead district to close the deal. A business meeting at her apartment—*right!?* We both knew what was really going to happen there. Interspersed between our sexual encounters that followed were conversations about a multi-million dollar trust fund she claimed to have, money she assured me would be more than enough to settle my debts and invest in the growing business. She spoke of not really loving her fiancé and of leaving him for me. We talked about traveling the world together and I fantasized living a jet-setting existence I'd only dreamed of with a beautiful woman. At the time, I'm not sure what the bigger hook for me was—the sex or the promise of riches and thus the power to do whatever I wanted to in a lifestyle without limits. The more I obsessed on this fantasy, the easier it was for me to justify leaving my wife and children behind for a better life. By this time, I had truly lost my way. I was engrossed in a delusional fantasy world of sex and greed.

Of course, I later discovered that all of the talk was just that—talk and empty promises. As it turned out, Teresa was a sham, a compulsive liar with a history of seducing naive men like me, men who were safely married and could easily be kept hidden out of sight. She used sex and charm and spun tales of fantasy to keep several of us entangled in the same web of lies. Years later I was able to better understand this pathological behavior as a type of sexual addiction that women are more prone to than men called love or relationship addiction. However, that was only after losing everything and realizing that I myself was a sex addict, and that this affair that I had started and wouldn't leave was not just an isolated event for me. It was the latest example of a lifelong history of risky sexual "acting out" behaviors, dating back thirty years to my first exposure to pornography as an eleven-year-old.

My Great Escape

Discovering pornography at that young age was an unforgettable yet contradictory experience for me. On the one hand, seeing a picture of a naked woman posing on the back of a deck of playing cards was instantly arousing to me. I still remember exactly what she looked like. The feelings I felt were unlike any I'd ever experienced before, as if a shot of adrenaline was coursing through my veins. There was no doubt; I liked what I saw and how I felt when I looked at porn. But at the same time, I felt guilty and ashamed for looking at pictures of naked women. Something inside of me told me this was wrong, and so I kept these dirty little secrets about myself hidden from others and tried to reason it all out on my own.

Over the years, as pornographic material became more and more accessible, I found myself adapting to a new sexual belief system that would end up influencing my view of what it meant to be a real man and what a real woman was all about. Real men in porn were always macho, sexually aggressive, sexual conquerors of women, and almost always degrading to women. Real women in porn had big breasts, a perfectly shaped body, were always hungry for sex (even if they said no, porn taught us they really meant yes), and willing to do pretty much anything just to please a man sexually. I also saw women in porn as being flighty, flirty, promiscuous, and typically not very smart. In other words, a woman's value to mankind was based mainly on her body shape and size, and her willingness and ability to please a man sexually. Probably the most significant message of all was that this hypersexual, male-dominated way of thinking about sex and women was supposedly normal, and anyone who didn't think so was ignorant and definitely not cool. This twisted logic would erupt in the midst of my dating relationships and even in the workplace in my first job out of school. To me, women at work represented, among other things, endless possibilities for a sexual encounter—a dangerous and risky attitude to bring into the world of work for sure.

Shortly after graduation I donned a three-piece suit and went to work for the IBM Corporation as an account executive. The year was 1980 and saying you worked for IBM was like saying you worked for the CIA. It was a big deal back then because computers were still a mystery to most people (the IBM PC wasn't introduced until 1981). As a result, my IBM business card made me a hot property on the night club circuit, and I took full advantage of it, continuing my quests for anonymous sex and one-night stands. Occasionally, I'd let my personal and work lives intermingle by sleeping with someone I worked with or had just met during our long out-of-town training classes.

Porn still played a part in my life as it always had, but I kept any magazines I had stashed away at home and rarely brought any pictures with me to work. Even though I knew a lot of the guys I worked with also looked at porn, there wasn't much tolerance for the material in the workplace. So I naturally kept my recreational pursuit of pornography to myself and separate from my work life. In time, I even started becoming more discreet about whom I dated from work. After all, this was IBM and there were high expectations and professional appearances to maintain.

I did pretty well in the five years I spent as an IBM account executive, successfully completing my two-year sales training program and qualifying for three 100% Clubs. Of course, the competitive culture within IBM at all levels was fierce. All 30,000 of my peers in sales started out just as convinced as I was that we were going to be CEO of the company one day. But after spending a couple of years immersed in the starched shirt world of Big Blue, I came to the realization that I was no longer one of them. I just didn't want it badly enough. About that time, while in Atlanta attending a product sales training class, I met the woman of my dreams coming off the dance floor of a night club. I immediately asked her to dance, and several dances led to a date, which later led to a long-distance relationship that culminated in marriage about a year later. I was clearly in love. And just like that, my life became our life. I shared everything . . . except my penchant for porn.

Until that point, I had been sexually active as a single guy and porn had been like the wallpaper in the background of my life. No one else knew or could see the role pornography played in my everyday existence, especially not my wife, Patty, or our respective families. As far as they were concerned, porn didn't exist in my world at all. It was a nonissue. And to her especially, I came off as this great guy with a great job and a promising career—definitely a rising star worthy of hitching her future hopes and dreams to. What she didn't know was that even while we were dating, I was compulsively pursuing porn and sex with others. Although I had convinced myself years earlier that meeting and marrying the woman of my dreams would alleviate my urges and quickly replace my appetite for pornography, our first year of marriage was nonetheless tainted by my slow realization that being in a committed marriage relationship was actually increasing my desire for the material. That came as a real shock to me, but I still felt my recreational use of porn was something I could continue to enjoy and manage, although I knew I needed to keep it under wraps lest she discover that I might be something less than her knight in shining armor.

Suddenly, after years of being able to carelessly keep and consume porn in the dorms and apartments I had lived in, my home would no longer be a safe haven. Once again, I found myself having to hide this sexual behavior, as I knew porn was a pastime I could never partake of with my wife. I didn't even have to ask. That left only one viable option for me. I would have to find a new safe haven, a place away from home where I could escape into my secret world without the fear of being discovered. I would have to find a way to use porn at work.

USING PORN @ WORK

If there were ever a good time to start using porn at work, 1983 was the year. My employer, IBM, had only introduced the PC a few years earlier, and it just so happened that I was the rookie sales rep in our office "selected" to be the PC product specialist. Few IBM sales reps took the product very seriously back then, including me. Everyone wanted to sell the "Big Iron"—expensive mainframe computer systems that filled entire floors of office buildings and sat perched on raised floors to accommodate the plethora of complex cables and cooling systems the behemoths required. The PC, on the other hand, was like a toy. It even fit on a desk. It was widely viewed at the time as a defensive move by Big Blue to check the advances in the education market of a small start-up company in Cupertino, California, called Apple Computers. I grudgingly took on the role of PC Specialist even though I was the furthest thing from a computer nerd that you could find. But while knowledge of the internal workings of these machines bored me, running the applications and learning about the miraculous things you could do with them that you couldn't do

- 20% of men and 13% of women admitted to accessing pornography at work.

- A 2004 study of 350 companies in the U.S., the United Kingdom, and Australia found that one-third of workers admitted passing along porn at some time—and half of all workers said they'd been exposed to sexually explicit material by co-workers.

on a terminal hooked up to a mammoth mainframe was something else altogether.

By the time I had returned to work from our honeymoon in early December 1983, I had moved on from my job as PC Specialist to bigger and better things at IBM. But during that time I had become pretty well versed at running a PC. Although the PC applications back then were limited to rudimentary electronic spreadsheets and word processors (the Internet was still over a decade away), I knew that product inside and out—knowledge that would come in handy when the PC started maturing and getting better at handling graphics-based applications. When it did, the techies I worked with started showing up with floppy discs and later with CD-ROMs loaded with high-resolution pornography. It was quite a step up from the plain old adult magazines I was used to, and this early version of computer-based porn couldn't have come at a better time for me—it was something you could only do on a personal computer at work.

While this new era of digitized pornography was taking hold, an even bigger development was taking place in our cubicle-bound workspaces. Having the personal computer on our desks at work made our time spent there much more private. Since corporations were still many years away from networking PCs together, those of us who were lucky enough to have them back then (only computer industry employees, executives, and CEOs used the first IBM PCs at that time due to their high cost) owned our own "islands of automation." We were the first to experience both the personalization and the new isolation inherent in this latest advance of the information age.

For me, my work computer quickly became my new repository for all things pornographic. Since I hadn't advanced to the ranks of having a private office with a door and the PC wasn't portable yet, perusing porn on a computer at work was still a risky endeavor—too risky to try from a cubicle during regular office hours. So even though I'd often have to engage in my "Great Escape" in the confines of my car or the men's restroom, drawing on the mentally stored images of the girls on CD-ROM, it was a far less risky option than trying to use at home with a wife and kids around.

A Safe Haven

It wasn't until the late '80s that my workplace finally became a safe haven for using porn at work. I left my job at IBM in 1985 when my wife and I decided to move to Atlanta to raise our family in closer proximity to hers. Plus, we had both had enough of the cold and dreary rain of Seattle. Two years later our first son, Christopher, was born, and shortly after that I went to work for NEC, a global giant in the world of computers and communications. It was there that I first started using a truly portable PC—a sleek executive notebook computer with all the bells and whistles of its time. I had also paid my dues in the industry long enough to have earned my own private office. That combination, mixed in with a lot of travel and the autonomy of a senior sales position, created more than enough opportunities to take a little time off here and there to pursue my Great Escape. The workplace had finally become my safe haven for porn.

For the first time, I started stealing big chunks of time from my employer in pursuit of my guilty pleasures. I would spend hours a day in the office and on the road engrossed in porn. The increased stress and pressures of first-time fatherhood and management responsibilities at work only added to the constant need I felt to find relief. Although I enjoyed being an active rec league coach and athlete, as well as spending time outdoors with my family, no other form of relief was more immediate or satisfying to me than fantasizing and masturbating to porn. I started building regular routines and rituals into my life so I could act out sexually in secret: midmorning in my office before making sales calls or meeting with employees; in my car while out for lunch, if I happened to be alone; late afternoon in the men's room when I needed a pick-me-up. Often it was a factor in my running late for meetings or coming home late at night. On some occasions it would easily add an hour or two to those nights when I really did have to work late, but not that late, at times even making the difference between being there to put my son to bed or not.

Traveling on business and staying in hotels brought even more unstructured time and less accountability, the perfect mix for acting out sexually. As a senior sales rep and later as a manager, I often traveled alone. In those cases, hotel rooms posed a dangerous doublethreat to me. Not only were the ubiquitous pay-per-view movies available, there was also the unique opportunity to play the role of voyeur.

Hotel rooms were only as private as their window draperies allowed them to be. Most of the hotels I stayed in were nicer, slightly upscale hotels that allowed plenty of privacy and protection for their guests from the wandering eyes of others. But occasionally I'd find myself in a room whose picture window was facing a whole building full of picture windows just like mine, with the curtains arranged in a variety of positions—some completely open, partially open, or open with only the see-through curtain liners closed. The array intrigued me as I recalled countless scenes from pornographic photo galleries and movies where the man is looking through the window of a hotel or a home at his neighbor's wife or daughter undressing in her room, a woman he would be having raucous sex with in a later scene. Echoing the views of Dr. Patrick Carnes, world-renowned expert in the field of sexual compulsivity and addiction, this scene held a special place in my mind's sexual- arousal template. It was a scenario that for some reason was more sexually stimulating to me than most others, so it was not all that unusual for me to seek it out. Of course, that didn't make it right, just more predictable.

Since hotels had yet to implement the practice of omitting the titles of pornographic pay-per-view movies from their guests' room charges, watching pay-per-view porn never went beyond the multiminute previews for me. However, the now defunct X-rated previews were more than enough to get me started in my acting out ritual.

Pretty soon my laptop was open and in went the disc, loaded with the latest and greatest porn that my resourceful tech support rep or systems engineer could find. Even when I tried not to do it, more often than not I'd give in, promising myself to only look for a few minutes. This inevitably led to a few extra minutes, then promises of stopping on the hour. Then the next half hour. It was a game I played with myself over and over again that I'd always lose at. I tried to convince myself that I was managing it, that somehow I'd earned the right to self-indulge. Maybe it was a celebration for making quota that month or for a successful business meeting earlier that day with a client. Other times it was to escape the guilt and frustration that came with failing to stop as I had promised myself I would. For whatever reason, I knew there would always be a next time just over the horizon. *So why not make that next time now?* I reasoned.

Using porn at work, while a big turn-on, was always a huge productivity drain. Still, nothing could even come close to the high it provided, along with chasing a few seconds of brief nudity as a voyeur. I spent hours on end on the edge of my bed in hotel rooms or standing just behind the curtain, peering into the darkness, waiting for the chance occurrence of seeing a woman undressing. Sometimes that meant waiting all night for the lights to go out in the last room in view. Oftentimes, my efforts were in vain as the curtains would be drawn or I'd discover that the room was empty or occupied by another traveling businessman.

All of this filled me with a great sense of shame and guilt about what I was doing and whom I had become. But those growing feelings of shame and self-hatred only made me long even more for a way to escape from the pain they caused. And when I was "lucky" enough to claim my prize and catch a brief glimpse of some unsuspecting woman unclothed in another room, the adrenaline and dopamine rush would literally make me shake. It was unlike anything I had ever felt, and those euphoric highs were enough to keep my hopes alive that a similar, even better buzz lie just around the corner. Thus my propensity for porn had turned a corner, and I started pursuing it in the form of live, real women. As realistic as you could get, or so I thought.

High-Speed Porn

Pretty soon, we started connecting our laptops to this new public network called the Internet. Here we could go well beyond the private local networks in our offices and tap into all kinds of geographically scattered data repositories. At first, it was all business as we started using this new productivity tool to do more in-depth research on our customers and competitors. Then, general news and novelty sites started appearing. Pretty soon, my always resourceful systems engineers and technical specialists, the guys who *really* knew how to use computers, were passing around links to Internet Web sites that were loaded with the same kind of high resolution pornography that I had been seeing on high-density floppy discs and CD-ROMs for years. But many of these sites were storing hundreds, then thousands of images. We were all thrilled and amazed at the unlimited potential that Internet porn sites appeared to have to entertain us.

In those days we were experiencing more than the usual amount of stress around our home. My wife, Patty, and I spent the latter part of the 1980s and the first half of the 1990s trying to conceive another child. We spent seven years going through in vitro fertilization before we got pregnant on our own with our second son, Andrew. He was truly a blessing and a wonderful child and we were thankful to God to have been given a second son. Still, the years of infertility treatments took its toll on our personal relationship as our physical and relational intimacy had been hijacked by the emotional highs and lows of failed fertilization cycles and preplanned basal temperature charts.

I left NEC in the late 1980s through a reduction in force and hopped around the industry for a while until I settled down to work at Unisys, another huge computer company. Once again, I had a sales job where I traveled a lot and had little accountability. By this time in my career, I had built a reputation as a solid, polished sales professional with the potential to be a great one. I always interviewed well and sold myself easily into choice, six-figure sales and management jobs with multimillion dollar quotas. My resume now included over a decade of sales awards and accolades. However, cracks were beginning to appear in my armor. I was not performing as well as my resume might have indicated since I was now spending inordinate amounts of time using porn at work instead of focusing on growing sales revenue for my employers. I was also becoming increasingly bored with work and the people I worked with. The real world couldn't keep pace with the escapism I enjoyed in my fantasy world. Even though I always had great jobs and worked with wonderful people, I was restless and looking for something more.

As my sales and management jobs became more demanding and stressful, I became more compulsive and impulsive about my use of porn at work and related sexual acting-out behaviors. Once again, technology seemed to rise to the occasion for me. While the Internet was changing daily and always beckoning with new fantasies, the highway to getting there was still a two-lane dirt road. Dial-up connections to the World Wide Web were agonizingly slow when it came to downloading the huge graphic image files that were the staple of

Internet porn. So when companies like mine started providing their employees with high-speed Internet connections directly from our offices to the World Wide Web, those of us who surfed the 'Net for porn were elated. The workplace was not only a safe haven for surfing porn, it was on the leading edge of high performance. No doubt this is one of the main reasons why 70% of all pornographic Web site visits occur between the prime workday hours of nine to five.

As the Internet was revolutionizing the sales profession by putting an unprecedented amount of information at our fingertips, it was also providing new opportunities for porn surfers like me. While our employers were beginning to talk of establishing acceptable use policies for those of us accessing the Internet at work, their motivation was mainly to protect themselves from the high cost of confidentiality breaches and loss of trade secrets. Meanwhile, we were swimming in a sea of porn, and more and more water cooler conversations revolved around new porn sites and erotic genres that had just been discovered. It was Sex Education 201 for those of us who had taken 101 back in the early days of print pornography. The exponential growth in the sheer volume of content that was there at our fingertips seemed surreal, and we all knew we could explore this new world easily, and affordably (more free content than you could see in a lifetime), but even more importantly to us, safely and anonymously. Until companies started clamping down years later with Filters and Internet Acceptable Use Policies, surfing porn sites at work really was a way of life for me and legions of my peers. The office had become our new "safe haven."

The tipping point for me came when the increases in network speed and bandwidth paved the way for streaming video, meaning that full-motion video clips of porn movies could be delivered right to your laptop. The impact that breakthrough had on me was both devastating and debilitating. It was like throwing fuel on the fire of my increasingly compulsive and addictive sexual behaviors. Streaming video also made possible real-time content from Web cams and other voyeuristic, CU-SeeMe technologies that essentially hit the bulls-eye of my sexual arousal template.

By the mid 1990s, my work resume was starting to resemble a slice of Swiss cheese. I was moving in and out of different jobs every one to two years now, largely due to my growing obsession with sex and porn. Great opportunities slipped away as my jobs began to feel like obstacles preventing me from pursuing my favorite pastime.

Eventually, I was able to talk my brother and his business partner into taking me on in spite of my being somewhat overqualified for the job from an income perspective. I was hoping by then that the change of venues would be good for me not just by eventually improving my financial lot in life, but also by helping me lower the job-related stress and pressure that I was under. But it didn't work out that way. Running a branch office was like running a franchise business and far more complicated and stressful than I had anticipated. And the increased autonomy as the boss in a small office of one only made matters worse. With over 3,500 miles separating me from any oversight and accountability that my brother and his partner could provide, I eventually took advantage of their trust in me and the vast amounts of unstructured time I had, the private office, and the easy access to Internet porn from work and while traveling. It's a wonder it took as long as it did for me to finally fall. After years of feeding myself a steady diet of highly toxic Internet porn, I had finally become addicted. My wife and boys had been taking a backseat to my selfish pursuits for a while before then in spite of my working hard to hide it. I was out of control by the time Teresa walked through that door. By then I was ready to give it all away, to trade in my wife and family and job and friends for whatever fantasy life she offered. She was porn with skin on to me, and quite possibly a shortcut to a new life of material wealth, or so I thought at the time.

Not long after my affair went public, my brother and his partner began to see that I was spending far less time tending to the needs of a rapidly growing branch office than they had expected. Although I helped their company break new ground and opened the door to later expansion of the business, the first branch under my management still barely made a profit. Once again, I oversold promises and underdelivered on performance, which was the true story of my work history. Fortunately, my brother's business survived and continued to thrive after what could have easily been for them a far costlier brush with my risky sexual behaviors at work.

At the time I started the affair with Teresa, it was clear that my good judgment was being seriously impaired. I was living a day-to-day addict's existence "in the bubble"—irrational, irritable, impulsive, highly emotional, dishonest, unreliable, and subject to poor decisionmaking. Some of the choices I was making and the things I was doing behind closed doors could have had legal ramifications for me and for the firm, opening them up to litigation risks and a potentially damaging lawsuit. My thought processes back then were anything but clear. Yet I was so sure at the time that I was in control, like a sloppy drunk who is convinced he can handle the drive home. By the time my brother and his partner were sitting before me in Atlanta to conduct the hard business of letting me go, I'm sure they felt like the cop who has just pulled over a drunk for a DUI. It's been over ten years since that day and although my brother and I are on good terms again, we have never really talked much about that day or the events leading up to it. Too embarrassing for both of us, perhaps. Definitely a sad chapter of our lives that we'd just as soon forget.

I wish I could say that my story was an isolated incident. It's estimated, however, that anywhere from 16 to 21 million Americans struggle with some form of sexual addiction. Some physicians believe it's the most rapidly increasing diagnostic category of mental illness in the nation, spurred on by an estimated 300,000 new cases per year of Internet porn addiction.[1] Others in the medical community continue to question the validity of the claim that one can actually become addicted to sex or porn. However, those of us and our spouses and loved ones who have suffered from it need no convincing, and neither do the millions of business owners, managers, supervisors, and co-workers who have experienced the collateral damage while working by our sides during the height of our addictions. They may not have thought that our erratic and unexplainable behavior was connected to such a thing at the time, but those of us who have come through to the other side understand it all too well. Only we know how sick we were, and how easy it could have been for matters to have spiraled even further out of control.

Regardless of how bad it might have seemed at the time, there is always someone out there we know who has fared much worse. Someone who didn't hit bottom soon enough. Someone who continued to push the limits of sanity until the damage done to themselves and others was massive and irreversible. Some of these stories make the headlines and cause the hearts of CEOs and business owners to skip a beat. "What if that happened in my organization?" they wonder. "What would we do? How would we survive?"

Those of us who have "been there" and shared our stories in the confidential confines of our recovery group meetings and therapy sessions know that it's the stories that don't make the headlines that would really make your toes curl—the everyday gambles and risky behaviors that would *really* keep CEOs up at night if they only knew. While most of us have hit bottom and know our day of reckoning has come and gone, we think about and pray for others we know who still live in the same fog of denial that once kept us blind. We wonder what their rock bottom will look like and who they'll take down with them—a spouse, a child, a family member, friend, or co-worker. Or an entire organization. It has happened many times before. And it's sure to happen again.

A PERFECT STORM

When I picked up a copy of *Fortune* magazine in May of 1999 and read the cover story, "Addicted to Sex: Corporate America's Dirty Secret," it felt like I was reading a page out of my own biography. The article documented case after case of businessmen whose careers were ruined due to what experts were calling "sexual addiction." One by one, their resulting erratic behaviors and poor decision making had shipwrecked their careers, not to mention their marriages and families.

It had been only six months since my divorce and I was still living in a fog of denial and rationalization. But this article's stories about addiction and recovery helped me to see through the fog just enough to take the next step toward finally separating the truth

• Worldwide sex industry sales for 2006 are reported to be $97 billion, more revenue than Microsoft, Google, Amazon, eBay, Yahoo!, Apple, Netflix, and Earthlink combined. China is the largest consumer with $27.4 billion, South Korea is second at $25.7 billion, Japan is next at $20 billion, and the U.S. is fourth highest at $13.3 billion.

• Comcast, the nation's largest cable company, pulled in $50 million from adult programming in 2003. The big hotel chains like Hilton, Marriott, Hyatt, Sheraton, and Holiday Inn all offer adult films on in-room pay-per-view television systems. Adult movies are purchased by a whopping 50% of their guests, accounting for nearly 70% of their in-room profits.

from the lies I had come to believe about myself and others. It was a painful process that culminated in my "hitting bottom"—awakening to the damage and consequences that *my* choices and *my* behavior had brought into my life and the lives of others near and dear to me. There was no one else to blame, no disease model (unlike some, I chose to see sexual addiction not as an involuntary disease but as a pathological condition resulting from poor, selfish choices I made), no scapegoat.

As I was being broken and humbled daily by finally having to face the consequences of my actions, I couldn't help but ask myself, "How in the world did I get here?" I've had ten long years of recovery since then to consider the answers to that simple question—answers that are more complex and involved than we'd like to think as tens of millions of Americans are now diagnosed with sexual addiction. To help me explain some of the larger societal trends and influences that have helped bring us to this point, I can only liken what I've observed to the formation and progression of a *perfect storm*. By definition, a perfect storm refers to the simultaneous occurrence of events that, taken individually, would be far less powerful than the result of their chance combination.

Thinking back on how the events of my life have unfolded leading up to my recovery, it certainly felt like I was being tossed about and pressed upon by several converging storm fronts—the ever-changing economic and societal trends that make up our current culture. These "fronts" are the atmospheric dynamics that form the setting for each of our stories. Becoming more aware of them allowed me to develop effective strategies for avoiding potential land mines and falling back into the dark chasm of addiction. Businesses and organizations would be wise to consider them as well in developing their own strategies for how they plan to deal with this growing workplace epidemic.

Addictions are unwanted habitual behaviors and dependencies, usually based on a set of false beliefs we hold about ourselves, others, and the world we live in. You can never hope to understand or overcome an addiction if you fail to recognize and seek to alter the contexts in which they flourish.

So this part of the book is all about context. But before we jump into how you can guard your business against the consequences of a potential fall, we're going to examine what's really going on here from a higher vantage point. The only disclaimer I'd like to offer is to remind the reader that my intention here is not to provide an exhaustive and unbiased perspective on these broad topics, each of which has already been dissected and written about extensively by experts in their respective fields. On the contrary, my goal is to provide a biased, highly opinionated commentary on each based on my own personal experience, giving my readers insight into what the world looks like through the lens of a recovering sex addict. I hope you will find this perspective valuable, in the same way a person in charge of bank security benefits from the wise counsel of a reformed career bank robber.

With that said, I'll begin by taking a closer look at the three major storm fronts that I see converging over our culture today. I believe that their simultaneous occurrence is giving birth to a perfect storm that will rain down serious social and individual consequences.

Storm Front #1 — Hypersexual Media

There's an old advertising industry saying that's been around forever—Sex Sells! I remember first hearing that phrase back in the late 1970s when I was taking a mass media business course in college. This was about ten years after the so-called Sexual Revolution took root in our country. As we searched through liquor and cigarette company print ads looking for cunningly disguised phallic symbols or the form of a woman's body hidden in a glass of ice, it dawned on me that while this might be a fun way to spend our time in class, it seemed pretty unnecessary in the overall scheme of life. I mean, if I wanted to see a woman's legs or breasts, I knew where to find them. And it wasn't on TV or in grocery store magazine racks.

It's clear that a lot has changed in a few decades. Radio, print, television, and now new media have always been aware of the competitive advantage they gained in using any and all things sexual as a way to grab and maintain their audiences' attention. But never before have they enjoyed operating in a social climate of such permissive sexual values and mores. The result has been an unprecedented rise in both the use and acceptance of increasingly pornographic depictions of sex in all forms of our mainstream media.

For example, one popular study on the amount of sexual content on basic cable television found that the number of sex scenes nearly doubled between 1998 and 2005.[1] The study found that 70% of all shows, excluding daily newscasts, sports events, and children's shows, include some sexual content, averaging five sex scenes per hour. Yet out of those shows with sexual content, only 14% included at least one scene with a reference to sexual risks or responsibilities. In other words, these weren't public service announcements warning people about the danger of AIDS. Acting much like pornographers in the adult entertainment industry, they are simply using sex to sell their products and services with little thought given to the possible negative consequences that might befall the consumer.

While literally thousands of studies conducted since the 1950s have demonstrated a link between viewers' exposure to media violence and their increased tendency toward violent behavior,[2] relatively little attention has been paid to the impact that increased exposure to sexual content—14,000 sexual images and messages that the average viewer is exposed to each year on television alone[3]—is having on the average American consumer. One recent study focusing on teens found that watching sex on television increases the chances a teen will have sex, and may cause teens to start having sex at younger ages.[4] But other than a few studies scattered here and there, attended by a lot of rhetoric claiming everything from no harm done to predictors of sexual criminality, most of what we know about the impact of our sex-saturated mainstream media on real people and relationships is anecdotal.

What I do know as a recovering sex addict is that the portrayal of sex on television and in other media have been and always will be key potential triggers for me that could lead to unwanted sexual behaviors. The growing prevalence of sexual images, innuendo, and objectification, even on basic cable, is a constant threat to my sexual sobriety. Song lyrics, music videos, reality TV shows, sitcoms, commercials, print ads, and even the covers of magazines at my local supermarket checkout are like land mines dotting the landscape of my life, waiting to explode under my feet should I choose to entertain them for too long.

But as I talk with today's youth and college students, who appear to be the real target of this growing industry with an insatiable appetite for profits, I notice that all of this comes as no surprise to them. The most common response I get when I ask them if they're aware of all of the titillating content swirling around them is "Sure, we're aware, we've been soaking in it for years!" But when asked how they think this mainstreamed pornography might be affecting them, most can only shrug their shoulders and are surprised to discover that what they've been consuming all these years is, by definition, pornography.[5] Like the proverbial frog enjoying a swim in what will soon be a boiling pot of water, all we really know is it's a good bit warmer in here than it used to be.

Storm Front #2 — Enabling Technologies

While our hypersexual media is busy painting us a picture of an increasingly pornographic world, the availability of enabling technologies is responsible for providing access to this wide world of adult entertainment—anytime, anywhere, and in practically any medium we choose. Creating images of people as sexual and sensual beings has always fascinated us since long before the advent of film and photography. Yet until recently it's been a niche market with significant barriers to reaching mass market consumers, including severe legal restraints, and an unseemly cast of characters content with living life on the lowest rungs of the entertainment industry.

But with a few key appropriations of technology, perhaps the most notable being the shift from expensive film production processes and theater distribution to the use of low cost VHS video, the marriage between porn and technology was consummated. It was a bold move that gave the porn industry access to the masses and their millions of home VCRs. As the industry grew in wealth and influence, they could afford to invest heavily in newer technology, pioneering or perfecting such breakthroughs as CD-ROMs, streaming video, and online payment systems. Fast-forward to today's digital world where new media content creation technologies and distribution processes are constantly reinventing themselves (think YouTube and MySpace), and you have an environment ripe for "technology of the masses, by the masses, and for the masses." New markets are now being created by porn consumers, not just porn companies. Suddenly, as in so many other business sectors battling to stay ahead of the technological game in order to survive, today's adult entertainment industry executives increasingly find themselves on the outside looking in as their customer base reshapes and redefines the marketplace for porn.

Today's technology consumers now have the ability to create their own porn. They can shoot it, act in it, brand it, package it, market it, and distribute it locally, regionally, or globally. All without the help, knowledge, or distribution channels of the commercial porn industry. The Internet, consumer electronics, and a host of other digital computer and communication technologies have made all of this possible. That and an independent consumer who is less willing to settle for prepackaged porn.

I had a front row seat in this evolutionary process while spending over two decades working in the technology industry. I was also an avid consumer and early adopter of technology-driven porn throughout that time. But none of the previous technologies compared to the exponential leap that the development of the Internet and the introduction of Internet porn represented in terms of the increased accessibility, affordability, and anonymity that one could enjoy while consuming the material. The commoditization of high-speed Internet access that followed was like adding wind and gasoline to an already spreading brush fire. It just took off, for me and about 16 to 21 million others who are now sexually addicted. This unique combination of attributes (accessibility, affordability, and anonymity), commonly referred to as the "Triple-A Engine"[6] of Internet porn, lends itself particularly well to the development of sexually compulsive and addictive behaviors since together they intensify, accelerate, and allow you to conceal online sexual behaviors.

To be sure, technology can bring good things to life. But the misuse or misapplication of it, whether by individual consumers or whole industries, means that some of us will arrive at our unintended destinations much quicker than others. Or to borrow from the ad-pitch phraseology of Madison Avenue: "Why wait thirty years when you, too, can have the same sexual addiction it took me decades to get in just a few short months?"

Storm Front #3 — Sociosexual Pathologies

In December 2003, Faith Popcorn, one of the most respected marketing trend experts in American business, was asked by the

Wall Street Journal to forecast the major trends in business for the coming year (2004). This was her response: "Porn will become the norm. Nothing shocks anyone anymore. Our shock button has been turned off and that is why advertisers are finding it hard to get their messages through. The whole country is desensitized. The media will continue to push the limits of what's acceptable."[7]

In addition to speaking volumes about the state of our hyper-sexual media, this prediction, which most will agree has come true, should serve as a warning sign to us all that as a society personified, we are a sick patient and getting worse by the minute. Within the life span of a single generation, things we once considered sexually unthinkable are now defended as matters of personal choice that demand tolerance, no matter how offensive they may seem. As the line of decency moves into new territory representing the more raw and extreme genres of porn, a new norm is forming in our collective societal conscience. We are increasingly becoming desensitized to the sexualization around us. We are growing numb to those things that once shocked us.

Take for instance the landmark studies on students that were held simultaneously at UCLA and St. Xavier College back in the mid-1990s. Both men and women were exposed to over four hours of erotic video (of varying types: soft, hard-core, etc.) and then asked to answer a set of questions meant to gage their attitudes toward sex crimes. Comparing their before and after responses to those same questions, all of the men who were tested proved to be more accepting of "rape myths" after viewing the videos (that is, myths that women who are raped "ask for it" or secretly enjoy the experience). Surprisingly, over half of the women were as well.[8] The women in these films were portrayed as insatiable and in need of constant sexual fulfillment, the norm in porn.

The Meese Commission report from the Reagan era bent over

backward to try to show a connection between consumption of pornography and sex crimes, rape, and murder. While sex crimes in general have certainly increased over the past twenty years, the overall predictions were a bit alarmist. Yet, there's undeniable evidence that the overwhelming majority of those who commit sex crimes have also had a long history of pornography use.

Then there's the other side of the equation. Academicians and sex workers alike will defend their conviction that there isn't nearly enough wide-open sexuality yet to liberate our repressive society. They carry the mantra of people like Alfred Kinsey, Hugh Hefner, and Larry Flynt who saw or see themselves on a mission to set America (or at least themselves) free sexually. Both camps can be oppressive if you spend too much time soaking in their ideology.

This is why I believe when it comes down to really understanding how far our sociosexual pathology has taken us, we needn't look much further than our own personal history, our own current sexual attitudes, and those of the people around us. Think of how your own sexual viewpoints, beliefs, and behaviors have changed in the past ten to twenty years. Most parents I talk with are shocked when I tell them what some teenagers and college-age kids are into sexually. And yet when I talk with college students and share with them what junior high and high school students are doing sexually, most of them are shocked too. "What? We don't even do that!" is a common response. The lines of decency and sexual integrity have shifted as old values are replaced by new ones. But at what price? How far can the boundaries be pushed before someone gets hurt? How does porn go from being someone's "hobby" to becoming a serious health hazard to themselves and others?

Part 2

Why They
Won't Stop

4

FROM HOBBY *to*
HEALTH HAZARD

Nearly forty years ago, I stumbled upon pornography for the first time. It was 1969 and I was eleven years old. About a year later, I started masturbating to pornography and porn-inspired thoughts of sexual fantasy. In essence, I was starting to form a "relationship" with the material whereby I would use it to alter my mood or state of mind. Whenever I was bored, stressed out, or depressed, or was just looking to escape and entertain myself, masturbating to porn and sexual fantasy was always an option.

Over the next thirty years, my relationship with porn ebbed and flowed.

• **Pornographers currently release over 13,000 adult movies per year—more than twenty five times the mainstream movie production. Every thirty nine minutes a new pornographic video is being created in the U.S.**

• **51% of U.S. adults surveyed believe that pornography raises men's expectations of how women should look and changes men's expectations of how women should behave. 40% of adults surveyed believe that pornography harms relationships between men and women.**

At times, it was a big part of my life and consumed a large part of my conscious thoughts both at work and at home. Yet at other times, it was practically nonexistent. Most of the time, it was just kind of "there," subtly present in the background of my life. For the most part I functioned as a normal, balanced human being. I was responsible, mostly hardworking, fun loving, compassionate, and a bit goofy—but not obsessive or compulsive about my sexuality or anyone else's.

When I did look at porn, I considered myself to be a recreational user, or hobbyist, of a rather harmless—albeit embarrassing—form of entertainment. It was my guilty pleasure and my rationale was that it wasn't hurting anyone. As far as I was concerned, it was a cheap, pleasurable form of entertainment that was my just reward after a hard day's work.

Sure, there were times when I would obsess over a picture or a person. And yes, I'd always hide from others the fact that I looked at porn. I thought that my wife, Patty, wouldn't approve of what I did in secret, and neither would my family, my friends, or my employer. In most people's minds, porn was still taboo and evoked images of a dirty old man slipping into a seedy X-rated movie theater wearing only an overcoat and shoes. Or the perverted Peeping Tom sneaking around the neighborhood at night, looking through people's windows to watch them undress. I knew I was neither of those things, but who would ever believe me or really understand or respect me if I told them what I did? It was better to just keep it a secret, or so I thought.

Crossing the Line

Over the years, getting access to porn became easier and easier. The more I fed my porn habit, the greater my desire to look at the material. Even when I wasn't looking at porn, I would sometimes catch myself thinking about sex and the images I had feasted on regardless of where I was or what I was doing. Sometimes I would get sexually aroused just at the thought of slipping off and looking at porn again or acting out sexually. As time went on, the lightheadedness, or high, I would normally feel when using porn and masturbating became less intense. Achieving the same level of sexual arousal was starting to take longer and required my looking at more stimulating or obscene images, and eventually substituting those images for real people. This was especially true when I traveled on business and stayed in hotels. As I described earlier, I could always count on having a line of sight from my room into other rooms with partially closed blinds or drapes. The adrenaline rush I got looking at the pictures on voyeur Web sites had always been stronger for me than with the other stuff I looked at, but it was stronger still when I became a participant in the act itself. While this sexual acting out behavior was clearly a violation of the law and could have brought about serious consequences as well as embarrassment to me, my family, and my employer had I been caught and arrested, **the reality is that I didn't start out this way.** Going from hobby to health hazard wasn't something that suddenly happened overnight either.

Looking back over my life, I've tried to figure out exactly when I "crossed the line" from recreational user into compulsive addict. Discovering and using Internet porn at work was like adding rocket fuel to my secret obsession. It was this added component that kicked things into high gear for me and kept my thoughts of fantasy energized. But it was when I started moving from passive viewer to active voyeur that I began sliding down the slippery slope of addiction—the unstoppable fall from grace one hears addicts speak of so often. That's when I passed the point of no return and my use of porn became a serious health and litigation risk to myself, my employer, and others. Nothing came close to the exhilaration, the high that I felt for hours on end as a voyeur/exhibitionist, and once I discovered it nothing could stand in my way of achieving it. Not my wife and kids or other family commitments. Not sales calls or business meetings or even reprimands from my employer. Not even the loss of my job for the resulting poor performance at work.

At this point I'm sure my managers became perplexed by the

changes in me and my apparent lack of motivation and increased irritability and arrogance. When they hired me they saw nothing but potential—an attractive, experienced, articulate sales professional who knew all the right things to say and do to convince them that I'd be their next star performer. But as I became increasingly distracted by thoughts of sexual fantasy while on the job, I started to check out from my work responsibilities and care less about my job performance, which, not surprisingly, began to suffer.

This is how it worked: From the very moment the thought of looking at naked women or acting out sexually entered my mind, I started to become sexually aroused. That sexual arousal and anticipation of even greater arousal would continue until I completed any of a number of rituals or routines that I knew would culminate in the relief of my having an orgasm. Using pictures in adult magazines, the overall high was mildly intense and relatively brief—typically lasting less than an hour. With porn videos on VHS tapes or DVDs, it was more intense but still relatively short-lived—a few hours at most. However, with the Internet and its breadth and depth of variety, from pictures to videos on demand, I could surf for hours on end and maintain a heightened state of sexual arousal that was oftentimes even greater than the relatively short-lived climax. It was just a better, longer high.

As a result, Internet porn represented a huge leap in the amount of time I would spend at work while not actually doing work. When my addiction to porn escalated to yet another level and began to include acting out voyeuristically in real life, the intensity and arousal was so strong that I could put myself on a low-grade high or buzz for days, even as I plotted out my future exploits. At times, I even noticed my hands and arms shaking mildly but uncontrollably once I was "in position" in my hotel room. Later, I would discover that the only thing that came close to this level and duration of intense sexual arousal was actually having a secret affair with another woman. The secrecy and deception that were required and the constant state of danger and high risk that I felt about possibly being discovered literally put me in a constant state of arousal.

Crossing the line from porn use as a hobby to a health hazard came about through a series of small events, a shift in my sexual attitudes and beliefs that would occasionally erupt as sexual acting out behaviors. It all took time, lots of time. I had been redefining my personal views about what was and wasn't acceptable sexual behavior since the time I was first aware of my own sexuality, not long before my first exposure to porn. Over the next twenty-five years, those actions and attitudes escalated into a self-destructive series of sexually compulsive and addictive behaviors, mostly acted on while in school or at work. In other words, it took me two and a half decades to become a sex addict and five more years for my life to unravel and become unmanageable enough for me to lose control.

As anyone who's ever lived or worked with an alcoholic or drug addict can tell you, recognizing that a person is an addict is not that difficult once he starts losing control and his life begins to fall apart. It can be a painful sight, like watching a train wreck unfold in slow motion. Hearing the excuses about another lost job or missed

> "'I had sex with hundreds and hundreds of women I met in travels and business. Some numerous times, some one time, some whenever I was in town.... I believe you will find a lot of people out there like me. Executives are usually driven, power hungry, and egomaniacs. Hard drinking and women are often part of our story,'" says Mac Henry, who spent most of his career in the chemical industry and is now chief executive of his own small technology company in Phoenix."
>
> Betsy Morris, "Addicted to Sex," *Fortune, May 10, 1999.*

assignment, bailing them out of jail, or just seeing them high and zoned out again are dead giveaways of addiction that even a child can recognize.

But that's alcoholism or drug addiction. What about sex addiction? What are the early warning signs? And how does a person become a sex addict to begin with? Early on, it's hard to tell. Usually, everything seems normal on the outside, save an occasional inconsistency in character or an isolated incident that the addict is quick to rationalize or explain away (I'll talk more about the most telling warning signs later). Like the time my wife asked me to explain how an adult magazine ended up in my briefcase and I acted dumb and flatly denied knowing how it got there. It was the only time in our thirteen years of marriage, before the affair, that she ever caught me red-handed in possession of porn. But as the CEO in our introduction mentioned when commenting on what it's like to deal with an employee caught red-handed looking at porn at work: "It's like [talking with] 10 year olds." We've learned how to use well-crafted lies to hide our secrets and prevent others from seeing what's really going on inside of us. And when well-crafted lies won't work, we resort to acting dumb and totally unaware of the wrong we've done. It's all part of striving to project an appearance of relative calm while the truth is that a growing tsunami is picking up steam far below the surface.

Understanding What Lies Beneath

To help us gain a better understanding of what goes on beneath the surface during that preaddictive state, I want to introduce a new term—*sexual compulsivity syndrome,* or "Sex Syndrome" for short.

Before I go any further, I want to clarify that Sex Syndrome is not an officially designated or recognized medical disorder or disease, any more than sexual addiction is. Rather, it's a phrase I've coined to describe a state or condition that clearly exists but that up until now has been largely ignored by the mental health community. I've used this term to describe a preaddictive state that an individual typically goes through on their path toward sexual addiction. But it doesn't apply only to individuals. Sex Syndrome can also describe a sociosexual pathology that affects a group of people or an entire society when the group or society as a whole predominantly exhibits its symptoms and characteristics.

Sex Syndrome, as I define it, is a pathological state we enter when our capacity for sexual enjoyment and intimacy decreases as our exposure to intense sexual stimuli (like Internet pornography) increases. It is a condition that involves behavioral, biological, and environmental factors, and taken to the extreme it can result in sexual addiction.

To understand Sex Syndrome, you first need a basic understanding of how the brain, the most powerful sex organ in our body, processes sexual stimuli. We now know, for instance, that there is a cocktail of chemicals in the brain that energizes attraction and sparks romance.[1] Moreover, those chemicals are totally different from the blend that fosters deep love and long-term attachment in healthy relationships.

One of those attraction/romance chemicals is dopamine, a neurotransmitter that creates intense energy, exhilaration, focused attention, and motivation to win rewards. It's triggered by, among other things, novelty, pornography, and sexual arousal. A different chemical, oxytocin, is a hormone that promotes a feeling of connection, bonding, and attachment. It's produced and released by the brain when we hug our spouses or children, and when a mother nurses her infant. There are also others, such as serotonin and adrenaline, that play more of a supporting role. But it is in this sandbox of love potions that pornography comes to play.

Physiologically, in normal "love" relationships with real people, we typically move along a continuum from the dopamine-drenched state of early attraction and romantic love through various stages of increased intimacy and bonding to (if we're lucky) the relative calm and quiet of an oxytocin-induced attachment. But if we use pornography on a regular basis to induce fantasy-driven orgasms, then we have, in essence, formed a "relationship" with porn that can never leave the attraction stage, since pornography is inherently an inanimate object that only stimulates dopamine production. There's no relational give and take here, no knowing and being known. For a consumer of pornography, it's only about taking and getting sexually aroused. Over time, as pornography and masturbation repeatedly trigger intense sexual arousal, our brain is producing more and more dopamine, keeping us trapped in an intense cycle that mimics, yet never leaves, the early stages of infatuation, romance, and lovesickness. But the brain has a limit as to how much sexual stimulation it will allow. Overstimulate the brain with dopamine long and often enough, and the brain responds by increasing its tolerance level for sexual arousal. The result is desensitization, a response similar to what an alcoholic or drug addict experiences after repeated use and abuse of their drug of choice.

> "'At the time there is an incredible adrenaline rush,' says [Marnie] Ferree. 'It's a connection that I found I couldn't replicate anywhere else. But immediately after that experience is over, I mean driving back home, there is this incredible let down and you're just in a wash of shame.'"
>
> Keith Morrison, "Battling Sexual Addiction," NBC News/Dateline NBC, February 24, 2004.

For the person experiencing Sex Syndrome, sexual stimuli is the "drug of choice" to induce dopamine production in the brain rather than an external, controlled substance like drugs or alcohol. As more "drugs" are required over time to achieve the same "high," the user starts seeking out new and different ways to become sexually aroused. For the budding alcoholic or substance abuser, that may mean using greater quantities of their drug of choice or switching to more potent drugs—beer to wine, wine to hard liquor, weed to cocaine, coke to crack or methamphetamine—to get the same high or exhilaration they're used to experiencing.

It works the same way for a sexual compulsive—progressing in quantity and/or intensity from magazines to videos, couple to group sex, soft-core to hard-core, or from just watching to actually becoming an active participant. The more a person feeds their growing appetite for sexually arousing material or other sexual experiences, the more it takes to become adequately sexually aroused. In the process, the boundaries of decency and what they consider to be acceptable sexual behaviors are crossed, reset, and crossed again as the compulsive repeatedly breaks promises made to himself to stop, then starts back up again in an effort to erase the pain of repeated failures to do so.

Sex Syndrome is a scary place to be because the user doesn't think of himself as someone who is unhealthy or sick or losing control, but in reality he is. They may fail in small measures to begin with, but these are failures nonetheless in the critical areas of self-control and self-management. As the user looks around our Porn Nation and sees others who appear to be handling it, who are seemingly able to consume porn and act out sexually without consequences, he continues to deceive himself and strives to convince others that he's just as normal and self-controlled as they are, and that his use of porn is just a harmless leisure activity. He'll defend his drug of choice to the death, telling others that there's nothing wrong with it, that it's totally benign, and that everyone's doing it. "It's a harmless form of cheap entertainment," he says when pressed. "Nobody's getting hurt." But he can't see the long, slow decline that has taken place in his own life. He doesn't see what's really happening because he's biased and far too invested in his lifelong relationship with porn to ever really want to quit. He's lost the ability to be self-aware and to give an honest appraisal of where he's at. He's becoming a liability to himself and those around him, including his employer, who at this point is probably still oblivious to the growing severity of his condition. So he continues to use and abuse the material and his employer's trust, still able to hide his tracks and bypass the various blockers, filters, and other controls set in place to protect him.

There's a key principle at work that underlies the slow, cancerous decline that is Sex Syndrome as well as its more devastating kin, sex addiction: **what you feed grows, and what you starve dies.** If you continue to feed the brain ever-increasing amounts and varieties of intense sexual stimulation, the craving for a dopamine-drenched high will continue to grow. At the same time, you're unknowingly starving yourself of what all of us really want and truly need—genuine intimacy, healthy and wholesome relationships, and relational and sexual integrity.

The brain's ability to increase tolerance levels as a way to prevent overstimulation creates another quandary for the typical user of porn. As users are constantly being fed increasingly pornographic forms of sexual stimuli in our hypersexual culture and media, they are continually reminded of the need to quench their growing sexual appetites. The result is an ongoing sense of sexual dissatisfaction that they usually respond to by either a) denying and suppressing their growing hunger and desire for sex, or b) seeking out new ways and methods of satisfying their sexual desire. As long as advertisers, marketers, and the porn industry itself continue to use edgier and more arousing sexual images and messages to sell their products, the ranks of those struggling with Sex Syndrome and sexual addiction will continue to grow. As our sense of belonging and desire to be accepted by others is being ignored and starved, our sense of self and significance also suffers. This increased isolation from genuine intimacy and real relationships is one of the unmistakable indicators of a downward spiral as Sex Syndrome gives way to sexual addiction. As the unmanageability of it all starts to sink in, it instills overwhelming feelings of shame and guilt that fuel the addictive cycle. Unhealthy sexual attitudes and behaviors have not only skewed the individual's moral and relational compass, but they've also started to provoke very real feelings of self-condemnation and low self-esteem, not exactly the attributes of a happy, well-balanced person and productive employee. If they haven't already begun to surface, work performance problems and other work-related issues are sure to follow.

Because Sex Syndrome and sexual addiction aren't currently recognized by the American Psychiatric Association as mental disorders and thus not covered by most employee health plans, it's tempting for businesses and organizations to simply ignore the very real threat that these two tangible and (in the case of sexual addiction) well-documented pathological conditions pose to businesses and employees alike. The additional tens of millions of people who are only experiencing the early or middle stages of Sex Syndrome are still operating as capable individuals very much in control of their relationships and work lives. We see them functioning well in every level of the organization. However, if those who are progressing into the latter stages of Sex Syndrome aren't acknowledged and offered the hope and resources for help that they need, the ante goes up significantly for all businesses that employ those trapped in the downward spiral of sexual addiction. Unfortunately, the odds of discovering who is addicted or most at risk before the damage they can cause is done become slim at best.

> **" 'It's just this 24-hour distraction,' Karen says. 'Like the shame that it causes, I feel like it just stole my soul.'"**
>
> *Keith Morrison, "Battling Sexual Addiction," NBC News/Dateline NBC, February 24, 2004.*

5

RECOGNIZING *a* SEX ADDICT @ WORK

A few years ago, I ran into an old friend I used to work with at a software company in Atlanta. After exchanging pleasantries, we started getting caught up on what we were each doing for a living. After he told me he was still working for that same software company, I started to tell him that I'm a full-time writer and speaker on the subjects of sex addiction, pornography, and the sexualization of the culture.

Once he had a chance to pick his jaw up off the ground and put it back into place (a common reaction), he started telling me a story about a recent employee of theirs who had just gotten fired after being caught and reprimanded twice in less than a month for watching porn at work.

> • 10% of U.S. adults admit to Internet sexual addiction, of which 28% are women.
>
> • At a 2003 meeting of the American Academy of Matrimonial Lawyers, two thirds of the 350 divorce lawyers who attended said the Internet played a significant role in the divorces in the past year, with excessive interest in online porn contributing to more than half such cases. Pornography had an almost non-existent role in divorce just seven or eight years prior.

"I just don't understand it," he continued. "I mean the guy gets caught by someone who sees him looking at porn in his office. So the IT department checks his computer and discovers he has a bunch of porn loaded on his hard drive. He basically almost loses his job over it."

Then my friend got a confused look on his face. "But here's what I don't get. Less than a month later, they catch the guy looking at porn again. But this time, he's used another employee's computer and logged on with their user name and password. Of course they found out it was him and fired him for it. What an idiot! I mean he had to know that he'd get caught. How stupid can you be!?"

Good question. And I'm sure to most people it's a logical one to ask. Shortly after that conversation, I was reading a blog where a computer network engineer was saying much the same thing about a guy in his office who had been looking at porn and kept getting caught and reprimanded until finally getting fired after the third go-round. "This guy had to be a complete idiot. He knew if he kept getting caught looking at porn that he'd lose his job, but he still did it anyway. I just don't get it."

What they're really saying is that they don't understand the mind of a sex addict at work. That lack of understanding puts them in company with the vast majority of Americans. Most of the people I've met and spoken with over the past decade have never heard of sex addiction and have no idea what it is. When I start to tell them my story and that I'm a recovering sex addict, I get a pretty wide variety of responses:

"Sex addict! Cool, I know a bunch of guys who are sex addicts. Ya know, they just have a higher sex drive than most people. In fact, I sometimes wonder if I'm not one myself."

"Sex addict! You know, I think my twelve-year-old son's a sex addict. I found porn on his computer the other day. That's the third time we've had to talk with him about it."

"Sex addict! C'mon, give me a break! There's no such thing. Just a bunch of people of weak character who lack self-control and want to blame it all on porn."

"Sex addict. Hmmm. So, you haven't messed around with kids

sexually or anything, have you?" they're usually saying that as they're backing away from me.

Then there are the other responses. Like the guy who freezes in his tracks like a deer in headlights as he listens intently to everything I say. Or the spouse whose eyes start to tear up until she (it's usually a woman but not always) gathers up the courage to say something about the hell she's been through living with a sex-addicted husband in denial. Or the occasional people who call or write or come up to thank me for what I'm doing, then share their own personal struggles with pornography and sexual addiction. Most of these people have survived the chaos and come out on the other side of the hopelessness that once defined their daily existence.

Over the past ten years that I've been involved in my own recovery from sexual addiction, it feels like I've seen and heard it all. But I'm sure I haven't. In fact, turn on the TV and you're bound to be just as surprised as I sometimes am regarding the latest headline or news story about yet another sexually oriented moral failure or deviant sexual offense. From Oprah Winfrey interviewing recovering sex addicts and their spouses while proclaiming to America that sexual addiction is our number one addiction, to a scattered number of sex therapists and psychiatrists who deny that such a condition even exists, there's a lively debate going on now about sex addiction and a wide range of opinions about it. All you have to do is follow the news and you'll see there's no shortage of sexually related stories of people behaving badly.

In spite of years of overwhelming anecdotal and clinical evidence, the American Psychiatric Association, the organization that publishes the *Diagnostic and Statistical Manual of Mental Disorders*, or DSM, has yet to officially recognize sexual addiction as a mental disorder. That hurts the estimated 16 to 21 million people in the U.S. who are sexually addicted[1] because the guide is used worldwide by clinicians and researchers as well as insurance companies, pharmaceutical companies, and policy makers to help determine which mental disorders deserve coverage by health insurance plans. Without its inclusion in the DSM, employers and their insurance companies who use this manual as a guide have been reticent to provide health insurance coverage to their employees for a mental disorder they can claim doesn't exist.

So is sexual addiction real or a mythological disorder? Some experts in the medical field who support its diagnosis describe it as being in many ways similar to other addictions, where the behavior or activity comes to be used as a way to manage mood or stress and may become more severe over time. Others claim it's a chemical addiction in which sex addicts become addicted to their own brain chemistry (mainly dopamine). Either way, those like me and my family and millions of others who have lived through the nightmare and continue to live with the consequences have little doubt that sexual addiction is both real and incredibly destructive.

I have vivid memories of my time spent "in the bubble" of my addiction to porn and sex, complete with the requisite outbursts directed at anyone who dared to interrupt my behaviors or question my activities. I've made incredibly stupid choices and stood before my co-workers and loved ones emotionless, ready to abandon them and, in the case of my family, discard fifteen years of marriage and two precious boys for a mirage of what I foolishly thought would be satiable sex. I've taken great risks of arrest and exposed myself and others to embarrassment, all for just one more high, one more rush of dopamine and adrenaline. Once you've been an addict and have spent a couple of years in recovery, you know your addiction is real and really dangerous. Once its risks and consequences are thoroughly understood, sexual addiction may one day be recognized as one of the most dangerous, if not the most pervasive, addiction of them all. But for now it is easily dismissed as nonsense with a curt joke or a flippant "boys will be boys." So what is it really?

What Does Sexual Addiction Look Like?

Sexual addiction is among the least understood of all addictions. Dr. Patrick Carnes, one of the world's foremost experts and pioneers in the area of sexual addiction and recovery, defines sexual addiction as any sexually related, compulsive behavior that interferes with normal living and causes severe stress on family, friends, loved ones, and one's work environment.[2] It's also been described as a progressive intimacy disorder characterized by compulsive sexual thoughts and acts.[3]

Others talk about it more in terms of having an unhealthy sexual dependency. The Mayo Clinic uses the phrase *compulsive sexual behavior* instead of sexual addiction and defines it as "an overwhelming need for sex" and describes a sexually addicted person as "so intensely preoccupied with this need that it interferes with your job and your relationships... You may spend inordinate amounts of time in sexually related activities and neglect important aspects of your day-to-day life in social, occupational and recreational areas. You

"A 42-year-old television producer in the Dallas area... began to surf porn sites on the web, it consumed him. Before long he found that instead of working on his documentaries, he was locking the door of his home office (so his wife wouldn't catch him) and spending seven hours of his ten-hour workday downloading porn and compulsively masturbating. 'My work was getting very, very stacked up. I lost prestigious jobs because of it,' he says. 'It was to the point of paralyzing my business.' He is now in recovery with Sex Addicts Anonymous."

Betsy Morris, "Addicted to Sex," Fortune, *May 10, 1999.*

may find yourself failing repeatedly at attempts to reduce or control your sexual activities or desires."[4] However you choose to define it, sexual addiction is seen universally as an unhealthy or pathological relationship between an individual and their sexual thoughts and behaviors.

The latest research in this field gives us clearer pictures of just who sex addicts are. It's estimated that 8% of men and 3% of women in the U.S. are sexually addicted. That adds up to about 15 million people who suffer from this condition.[5] Other estimates put the number slightly higher at 6 to 8% of the population, or 16 to 21 million people.[6] Either way, that's a lot of people—about the same number as those who struggle with alcoholism.

Sex addicts come from every ethnic, religious, and socioeconomic background. Most come from severely dysfunctional families. Eighty-seven percent belong to a family where at least one other member of the family has another addiction.[7] Research has also shown that a very high correlation exists between childhood abuse and sexual addiction in adulthood. Ninety-seven percent of sex addicts reported experiencing emotional abuse, 83% sexual abuse, and 71% physical abuse.[8]

While sexual addiction is generally believed to primarily affect men, research by Dr. Patrick Carnes shows that approximately 20%

> **"One Tucson small business owner started sleeping around in high school after she was forced into sex on a date at age 14. 'I kind of felt like I had a male ego. I saw myself as the aggressor. It's a big power-lust game.' That didn't help her business. Sometimes she would ruin professional relationships with businessmen by sleeping with them... She finally ended up in a relationship with a man she believes was a sociopath; she is convinced she'd be dead by now had she not eventually joined Sex Addicts Anonymous."**
>
> Betsy Morris, "Addicted to Sex," Fortune, May 10, 1999.

of all patients seeking help for sexual dependency are women. (This same male-female ratio is found among those recovering from alcohol addiction.) As once was the case with alcoholism, many people cannot accept the reality that women can become sexual addicts. One of the greatest problems facing female sexual addicts is convincing others that they have a legitimate problem.[9]

Indicators of Sexual Addiction

So how do you know if you or someone you love or work with suffers from sexual addiction? While an actual diagnosis for sexual addiction should be carried out by a mental health professional, the following behavior patterns compiled by Dr. Carnes can indicate its presence.[10]

1. Acting out: a pattern of out-of-control sexual behavior.
Examples may include:
- Compulsive masturbation
- Indulging in pornography
- Having chronic affairs
- Exhibitionism
- Dangerous sexual practices
- Prostitution
- Anonymous sex
- Compulsive sexual episodes
- Voyeurism

2. Experiencing severe consequences due to sexual behavior, and an inability to stop despite these adverse consequences.
Some of the losses reported by sexual addicts include:
- Loss of partner or spouse (40%)
- Severe marital or relationship problems (70%)
- Loss of career opportunities (27%)

- Unwanted pregnancies (40%)
- Abortions (36%)
- Suicidal obsession (72%)
- Suicide attempts (17%)
- Exposure to AIDS and venereal disease (68%)
- Legal risks, ranging from nuisance offenses to rape (58%)

3. Persistent pursuit of self-destructive behavior.
Even understanding that the consequences of their actions will be painful does not stop addicts from acting out. They often have a willfulness about their actions, and an attitude that says, "I'll deal with the consequences when they come."

4. Ongoing desire or effort to limit sexual behavior.
Addicts often try to control their behavior by creating external barriers to it. For example, some move to a new neighborhood or city, hoping that a new environment removed from old activities will help. Some think marriage will keep them from acting out. An exhibitionist may buy a car in which it's difficult to act out while driving.

Others seek control over their behavior by immersing themselves in religion or their work, only to find out that while these compulsions may soothe their shame, it does not end their acting out.

Many go through periods of sexual deprivation during which they allow themselves no sexual expression at all. Such efforts, however, only fuel the addiction and address the symptoms rather than the root problem.

5. Sexual obsession and fantasy as a primary coping strategy.
Though acting out sexually can temporarily relieve addicts' anxieties, they still find themselves spending inordinate amounts of

time in obsession and fantasy. By fantasizing, the addict can maintain an almost constant level of arousal. Together with obsessing, the two behaviors can create a kind of analgesic "fix." Just as our bodies generate endorphins—natural antidepressants—during vigorous exercise, our bodies naturally release peptides when sexually aroused. The molecular construction of these peptides parallels that of opiates like heroin or morphine, but is many times more powerful. Of course, increased production of dopamine and adrenaline are also powerful reenforcers of their sexual acting out behaviors.

6. Regularly increasing the amount of sexual experience because the current level of activity is no longer sufficiently satisfying.
Sexual addiction is often progressive. While addicts may be able to control themselves for a time, inevitably their addictive behaviors will return and quickly escalate to previous levels and beyond. Some addicts begin adding additional acting out behaviors. Usually addicts will have three or more behaviors that play a key role in their addiction—masturbation, affairs, and anonymous sex, for instance.

In addition, 89% of addicts reported regularly "bingeing" to the point of emotional exhaustion. The emotional pain of withdrawal for sexual addicts can parallel the physical pain experienced by those withdrawing from opiate addiction.

7. Severe mood changes related to sexual activity.
Addicts experience intense mood shifts, often due to the despair and shame of having unwanted sex. Sex addicts are caught in a crushing cycle of shame-creating and shame-driven behavior. The few moments of euphoric escape into sex create strong feelings of shame that then drive the addict to find sexual escape once again.

8. Inordinate amounts of time spent obtaining sex, being sexual, and recovering from sexual experiences.

Two sets of activities organize sex addicts' days. One involves obsessing about sex, time devoted to initiating sex, and actually being sexual. The second involves time spent dealing with the consequences of their acting out: lying, covering up, shortages of money, problems with their spouse, trouble at work, neglected children, and so on.

9. Neglect of important social, occupational, or recreational activities because of sexual behavior.

As more and more of addicts' energy becomes focused on relationships that have sexual potential, other relationships and attributes—family, friends, work, talents, values—suffer and atrophy from neglect. Long-term relationships are stormy and often unsuccessful. Because of sexual preoccupation and intimacy avoidance, short-term relationships become the norm.

Sometimes, however, the desire to preserve an important long-term relationship, with spouse or children for instance, or to keep a job, can act as the catalyst for addicts to admit their problem and seek help.

In my own life, I exhibited every one of these behavior patterns at one time or another, and all of them simultaneously while I was addicted. Of course, in the midst of my addiction, I was in denial that most or any of these symptomatic behaviors were either present or all that serious. But as my disorder progressively got worse, the symptomatic behaviors became more pronounced to family and friends, as did the related consequences. The existence of one or more of these behavior patterns could point toward any of a wide variety of causes or mental disorders. However, taken together as symptomatic behaviors in one individual, the probability that a sexual addiction exists is quite high.

Telltale Signs of a Sex Addict @ Work

So what signs should an employer watch for that might indicate that their employee is struggling with sexual compulsivity and addiction (including Internet porn addiction)? Here are a few of the more visible behavioral clues (though these may indicate problems other than sexual compulsivity or addiction as well):

1. Hiding Internet use or secretive behaviors — As the Internet becomes a major part of their acting out rituals or routines, addicts become increasingly secretive about how and when they use it. Hiding or erasing Internet browser history files and cache memory records of site visits; positioning their computer screen in ways to guarantee personal privacy; utilizing software that switches their screen to a dummy spreadsheet or other application with one keystroke should anyone walk by; attempted use of certain spy-protection, anonymizer software (which gives a false alias for visits to illicit Web sites); and turning off site security controls are some ways in which an employee may attempt to conceal their behavior. Eventually, as their lives become more and more unmanageable, addicts will become sloppy when trying to cover up their trail. This often means that by the time a manager or co-worker catches them in a slipup, they've probably been breaking Internet-use policies for a long time and were just never caught.

> **"Researchers and psychologists who study Internet users' behavior say those who view online porn at work are doing so because they get a rush out of taking risks, engage in self-delusional beliefs that they won't get caught and, in some cases, suffer from addictive behaviors."**
>
> *Stephanie Armour, "Technology Makes Porn Easier to Access at Work," USA Today, October 17, 2007.*

2. Declining work performance — Obviously, this could be due to a wide variety of reasons, but the addict will *always*, at some point, begin to miss important deadlines, become habitually late to important meetings or functions, or overcommit himself or herself to tasks that they eventually leave undone or do poorly. In essence, they have placed their "drug of choice" in the position of their highest priority, meaning that any impulsive behavior that feeds their addiction trumps their felt need to work on an important presentation or complete work assignments that they know are important to their business. When this happens in a large organization with an employee further down in the ranks, the negative consequences of the misconduct can often be hidden to some degree and rationalized or justified with any number of lies. If they feel like they can hide their declining job performance from others, they'll continue to operate that way. But when the addict is a department head, executive, or business owner, the ramifications to the overall organization can be catastrophic, especially when the individual is a powerful figure who is surrounded by people who aren't willing to challenge them on their errant behavior until something very public happens and it's too late.

3. Withdrawing from others — As the addiction progressively gets worse, addicts prefer to be alone to act out or obsess on the object of their addiction in anticipation of their next "fix." As a result, those close to them will start to notice a change in their social behavior, the desire and need for them to spend more and more time alone and an increase in the amount of time that they can't legitimately account for. This is in part related to the increased amount of shame and guilt they feel about their unwanted behaviors and their inability to stop. In the workplace, this behavior can easily be misinterpreted as someone acting like they think they're too good to hang

around with other co-workers, or always having something pressing that they need to do instead of socializing on the job or at company functions. Especially when these behaviors signal a change in personality where a normally social and outgoing individual starts to withdraw, it's almost always an indicator that something is wrong. And even when they are present around others, addicts will often seem distracted or distant. These withdrawal symptoms will appear the strongest to his or her family as their loved one starts to "check out" from everyone close to them in order to live their lives immersed in their fantasy world.

4. Increased irritability — Along with withdrawal, an addict will also typically display an increased irritability and arrogance. Quite simply, they'd rather not be interrupted by "less important" activities, like doing their jobs, spending time with their spouses and children, or maintaining good health. At work, these people develop increasingly short fuses and become very defensive at the mere suggestion that something might be wrong with them. They are living in denial and can be very difficult to help at this stage, often opting for reprimands by a manager, quitting, or getting fired rather than taking advice from others to seek help or get counseling.

5. Losing sleep and declining health — Addicts at work spend an inordinate amount of time and energy—mental, physical, and emotional—in activities related to their acting out behaviors. It often grows into an "every waking minute" kind of obsession that invariably affects their health and even their sleep patterns. So addicts will often look run-down and tired, become overweight and out of shape (or anorexic and unhealthy), yet they'll keep moving and deny that anything is wrong.

6. Declining interpersonal skills — Oftentimes, someone who becomes addicted will show a confusing decline in their interpersonal skills. Usually masters of deception and world-class pathological liars, this characteristic will start to show itself more and more as their lives become increasingly unmanageable. Appearing distracted and exhibiting disinterest in other people's lives, pressing business issues, or impending deadlines, addicts are always moving toward total self-absorption. Over time, it shows in their loss of patience and a growing inability to connect with others.

7. Inappropriate sharing of sexual beliefs — One hallmark of this increasing self-absorption and loss of connection with others is an addict's blatant sharing of their own distorted sexual beliefs, as if to win over converts to their pornographic worldview of sex. This is often exhibited through personal conversations about sex, sexually oriented emails or materials being sent or forwarded to others, sexually themed chat room conversations, sharing pornographic images with others in person while at work or when traveling (to gauge their reaction), or even making sexual advances to strangers, co-workers, customers, and/or suppliers. Addicts are always looking to increase their fan base in the hopes that it will lessen their own sense of guilt and shame.

While these are just a few of the telltale signs of an employee's growing problem with sexual compulsivity and addiction and are certainly not exclusive to sex addicts, the presence of four or more of these showing signs within a six-month period of time is a strong indicator that this individual may have a serious problem and may require help or intervention.

Understanding the Cycle of Addiction

Addicts live in a cycle of addiction. They have all tried to stop numerous times and failed. I know because I did the same thing many times over. And although each time I promised myself I would stop, sooner or later I'd start back up again. This is the typical story of an addict. Their behavior generally conforms to the following predictable cycle:[11]

Preoccupation – the addict becomes completely engrossed with sexual thoughts or fantasies. Often I would "zone out" as I was engrossed in thoughts of fantasy, even when I was at work and other people were nearby. If this happened while I was alone, it was easy to lose track of time. A half hour became an hour, and one hour turned into several. At times, while preoccupied with sexual thoughts, I would suddenly come to realize I was late for a business meeting or had missed an appointment. In that case, I would typically resume my sexual thoughts or fantasies after the "interruption" was over and I was alone again to indulge once more.

My preoccupation time quite often cut into meeting preparation time or time I had set aside for other important activities related to my work or personal life. When I was involved in the affair, my preoccupation with thoughts of an impending rendezvous or some other planned time together rendered me pretty much useless at work. In order to make more room for this "time away," I would often put off important work responsibilities, telling myself I'd get to them later when I seldom actually would. If anyone at work caught me in this distracted state, I would quickly respond with a lie or fabricate a story to guard my secrets.

Ritualization – the addict follows particular routines in a search for sexual stimulation, which intensify the experience and which may be more important than reaching orgasm. I had many rituals and routines, all very specific and planned out. Some rituals consumed me and required that I ignore or block out everything else in my life—my job, my wife and family, other obligations. Many rituals were simply integrated into other daily routines, like checking out Internet porn sites after first reading my work email, or revisiting those porn sites and printing out certain pictures before leaving the office for home.

There were also certain "triggers" that would set my ritualization behaviors in motion. Back in the early days of the Internet, it was that irritating sound of a dial-up modem making a connection. To me, that meant gaining access to the Internet and surfing porn sites was just moments away. Of course, waiting around for the images to finish downloading at two mph was agonizing. Another trigger was checking into my hotel room. Yet another was coming to the end of the workday and saying good-bye to the last person leaving the office. That meant I was alone and free to act out. Sometimes, something as simple as closing my office door was a trigger to preoccupation and ritualization, because closing that door was something I did when I masturbated to porn alone in my office. Even if I was simply closing the door to meet with a manager or a co-worker, it still reminded me of my next workday ritual and opportunity to act out.

Compulsive sexual behavior — the addict's specific sexual acting out behaviors. Examples of these are compulsive masturbation, indulging in pornography, having chronic affairs, exhibitionism, dangerous sexual practices, prostitution, anonymous sex, compulsive sexual episodes, and voyeurism. This is the area where you play a game with yourself regarding what you deem to be acceptable and what is "out-of-bounds" behavior. The more you expose yourself to certain sexual acting out behaviors, the more compulsive and desensitized you become to past behaviors. And the more desensitized you become, the more apt you are to cross the line into new behaviors you once considered unacceptable.

There was a day early in my career when I swore to myself I'd never bring porn to work. Then, after I started buying magazines while on business trips, I promised myself never to bring it into my office. Failing there, I then loaded porn on my work computer, again after promising myself I would never do it. That progressed to sleeping with other co-workers, then acting out sexually as a voyeur while staying in hotels on business trips, then later to acting on exhibitionist fantasies, and on and on. Every time I crossed a new line, I'd rationalize it by trying to make myself feel good about what I *wasn't* doing—prostitutes, massage parlors, group sex, etc.

Despair — the acting out does not lead to normal sexual satisfaction, but to feelings of hopelessness, powerlessness, and depression.

In my case, my sales performance was a major determinant of my income, so as I invariably began to falter and fail, the feelings of guilt, shame, and despair that would always come rushing in on me immediately after acting out were intensified even more. I would despise myself for what I had done and what it had cost me, and I always made a promise to never do it again. As I wrestled with intense negative feelings of self-hatred and disgust, I would start to escape by becoming preoccupied with a whole new series of sexual fantasies. There was always a trigger or something just around the corner that would con me into thinking that this time my Great Escape would take away the pain for good.

To be sure, sexual addiction is controversial, and it is important to realize that some people latch onto this label as a crutch instead of accepting personal responsibility for the choices they've made in life, choices that have hurt themselves and others. A lot of people assume that all addicts cling to the "addiction is a disease" mantra as a way to avoid accepting responsibility for their selfish actions and poor decision making. While that is often true for addicts who are in denial or those who might be early in the recovery process, most recovering addicts I've met, including sex addicts, are quick to acknowledge that they're ultimately to blame for their lot in life.

However you view it, sexual addiction or sexual compulsivity or whatever you choose to call it is a very stark reality for millions of men and women across this country and throughout the world.

For some, it's a living hell that instills intense feelings of hopelessness and helplessness in the face of our society's onslaught of sexual images and messages. For others, it's been an important part of a lifelong journey toward rediscovering an important part of themselves that went missing long ago. We've learned a difficult lesson on the importance of having self-respect and respecting others. For those of us on the other side of hopelessness, it's taught us valuable lessons about who we are not just as sexual beings but as whole human beings—physical, emotional, sexual, relational, and spiritual beings who possess an immeasurable capacity to rise above our circumstances in order to remake ourselves into better people. We are the ones who chose to get well, and now we have a story to tell and a message of hope to share with those who may be waiting. Waiting to see when it'll be safe to come out of hiding and face their demons once and for all.

That is exactly what I have been doing for the past five years as I've been traveling around the country and throughout the world sharing my story and what I've learned along the way about this "disease of the heart" with the people I feel need to hear this message the most—college and university students. Because as they stand on the precipice of making their own history and forging their own way of life, I believe we owe it to them to tell them the truth about love, sex, relationships, and porn. We have immersed this group of next generation leaders, what some refer to as the Millennial Generation, in more sexual imagery and marketed more sexual messages their way than any other generation in history. We've sold them sex in their movies, their music, their video game characters, their clothes, cartoons and TV shows, and soft drinks . . . then we wonder why they struggle with sex, love, and relationships.

So now I'd like to draw on my experiences of the past five years, having met with and spoken to college students on over 150 college campuses on two continents. Not only have I shared my story and my time with them, I've also given them an opportunity to talk back and to share what they and their peers are really doing, saying, and thinking about sex and porn—over 25,000 voices sharing their sexual beliefs, attitudes, and behaviors.

Readers and prospective employers alike, I present to you the workforce of tomorrow and the future of our great nation—the graduating class of Porn University.

The Graduates *of* Porn U: TODAY'S WORKFORCE

In the past as I traveled throughout North America and parts of Europe giving my Porn Nation presentation, we always used the standard tools to promote the event including posters, flyers, newspaper ads, and table tents. But as my curiosity started to rise about where students were really at regarding their sexual attitudes, beliefs, and behaviors, we decided to ask them to take a short, informal "sex survey." What started out as a promotional tool quickly evolved into an unscientific yet revealing empirical study. After starting out in our first few events with a makeshift written survey of random questions I had created, I began thinking about a sexual addiction screening test I had found on the Internet (www.sexhelp.com) and taken many years before when I was trying to determine whether or not I might really be sexually addicted. It was developed by Dr. Patrick Carnes, a psychologist who had written many of the books about sexual addiction I had read early in my recovery. Dr. Carnes

• A study of university computer networks by Palisades Systems found searches for child pornography at 230 colleges nationwide. The research revealed that 42% of all searches on file-to-file sharing systems involved child or adult pornography.

The study also found that 73% of movie searches were for pornography and 24% of image searches were for child pornography; only 3% of the searches did not involve pornography or copyrighted materials.

was a pioneer of sorts and his first book, *Out of the Shadows*, had been recommended to me more than any other book on the subject. The SAST was originally designed to serve as an early screening diagnostic tool that counselors, therapists, and other medical professionals could use to help determine the degree of compulsivity and the extent of addictive sexual behaviors that a patient might be exhibiting. Since this test was actually a brief survey of twenty-five yes/no questions that the respondent could complete on their own, it seemed like the ideal "sex survey" to use not just for promotional purposes, but to give students immediate feedback regarding the level of risk that their responses might be an indicator of and suggestions on an appropriate course of action.

In the spring of 2005, we got permission from Dr. Carnes to put a copy of the SAST on our Web site (www.pornatworkthebook.com) and use it to survey the students and help promote our events. We promised to maintain confidentiality and protect the respondents' identities. The positive response of students was encouraging and continues to be overwhelmingly supportive of what we're trying to do. We've since analyzed the survey results from tests taken beginning in the spring semester of 2006 through the spring semester of 2008. During this time period, 28,798 people took our online SAST, 93% or 26,782 of whom were currently enrolled as college students at the time (the rest were faculty, staff, or others who were a part of the campus community). What follows is a brief summary of some of the key results and findings that I found to be most relevant to today's employers as they size up the newest members of the workforce. For readers interested in a much more thorough and detailed analysis of all of the study results, I encourage you to pick up my book *Porn University: What College Students Are Really Saying about Sex on Campus.* I also recommend that you visit the Sex Survey page of our main Web site at www.pornnationthebook.com for additional study information and statistics.

First Exposure and Online Sex

The majority of college men who took our survey were first exposed to porn long before they entered high school, typically somewhere around the age of puberty or shortly thereafter. A third of them were first exposed via the most toxic distribution pipeline we know of, the Internet. I say toxic because you're always only a few clicks away from sampling images and video depicting anything from the mildest nude images to the most obscene "money shots" ranging from fetishes and bestiality to violent rape and even child pornography. Scenes and images the mind is not likely to soon forget, if ever.

As for college women, most weren't exposed to pornography until later on in their teenage years, and at least a third were exposed after they turned 16. And while it's a fact that more and more women are reporting that they struggle with their thought life because of their early exposure to the material, far more have a "take it or leave it" attitude toward porn and the guys they know who are into porn.

> **"I have more memories of porn than of childhood."**
>
> *Troy, 25, a college student who was 12 the first time he saw pornography on the Internet.*
> *"The Cyberporn Generation," People, April 26, 2004.*

While both genders were very similar in the amount of time they were spending on the Internet, when it comes to pursuing sex online, college women and college men could hardly be more different. Here's the breakdown:

Hours Spent Online / Week	Men	Women
Less than 5 hours	10%	11%
5–20 hours	52%	57%
21–50 hours	30%	27%
50+ hours	8%	6%

Hours Spent Online / Week for Internet Sex	Men	Women
0 hours	36%	82%
Less than 5 hours	51%	16%
5–20 hours	11%	1%
Over 20 hours	2%	1%

Eighty-two percent of the college women we surveyed say they spend 0 hours per week online for Internet sex, while only 36% of the guys claimed that they don't spend any time at all pursuing sex on the Web. Yet while 51% of the guys admitted to spending at least up to 5 hours a week online for Internet sex, just 16% of all college women did. And only 1% of college women said they spent more than 5 hours a week online for sex, but a whopping 11% of guys spend 5–20 hours and another 2% spend over 20 hours a week—six times as many men as women participating in online sex in the heaviest use categories.

In spite of the best efforts of the adult entertainment industry to reach a largely untapped female audience, the overwhelming majority of college women (82%) have decided they can live without it and for the most part just ignore it. Their primary education about sex, love, and relationships is clearly coming from other sources. But take a closer look at the average college male and you'll see that nearly two-thirds are pursuing a relationship with porn and cybersex to varying degrees of frequency and intensity. No wonder it's common to hear female college students say, "All of the guys on campus look at porn."

What most guys started doing secretly at an early age, they now pursue openly and without reservation while in college—a clear response to their newfound sexual freedom. This in contrast to what they'll experience once they enter the workforce upon graduation—a "zero tolerance" world that will require them to once again hide their rather public sexual attitudes and behaviors. But will it be that easy for them?

Women and Sexual Abuse

If consuming porn is part of the legacy of being a college male, then being a sexual abuse survivor is in many ways the hallmark of college females. When asked "Were you sexually abused as a child or adolescent?" 5% of the college men answered "yes" while more than twice as many college women, or 12%, admitted that they were sexually abused earlier in life. So why is this important? Dr. Patrick Carnes observes that studies show a high incidence of sexual addiction among people who were victims of sexual abuse, incest, and other sexual trauma early in their childhood.[1] Many of those same men and women go on to sexually abuse themselves (through porn and harmful sexual behaviors) or others, including spouses and children.

It's hard to emphasize enough just how important this statistic is. Initial childhood and adolescent sexual experiences involving exposure to pornography or being sexually abused have a way of leaving a permanent impression on more than just a person's memory. They traumatize our very souls and damage our spirits, branding individuals for life in many of their own minds as "damaged goods."

The resulting self-hatred and self-condemnation form the very foundation of a faulty belief system common to all addicts. Whether it's believing that sex equals love (as in the case of incest where a parent tells a child that by having sex with him, the parent is simply expressing their love for them), or believing that no one would love them if they ever knew everything about them (as in the secrets a sexually abused child is often forced by his abuser to keep, or the guilt and shame children carry with them after early exposure to porn), abuse victims face a lifetime of struggles with self-esteem, self-image, and body image issues as well as having difficulty building trust and maintaining healthy, intimate relationships with others. Manifest in the workplace, these individuals often need help in order to function normally in healthy relationships with others and often "act out" in some of the sexually inappropriate ways we have already discussed.

With women dominating this sex abuse statistic in our survey's results by more than a 2 to 1 margin over men, it should come as no surprise that our survey also shows that more than twice as many college women as men admitted to staying in romantic relationships after their partners became emotionally or physically abusive—23% of women versus 10% of men. That's 1 out of every 4 women on campus compared to only 1 in 10 men, roughly the same number of women who fall victim to rape while in college. The survey results also indicated that men were much more likely to be the abusers than women.

When you combine these findings with the fact that a large majority of college males have been regular consumers of pornography since before many of them entered puberty, and typically at an earlier age than the girls, it's not hard to see why this might be a dangerous combination in the workplace. Those with a history of sexual abuse (as either the victim or the abuser) have a greater risk of becoming sexually addicted. As a result, they're also more likely to be involved in unwanted sexual behavior—especially with another abuser or victim of abuse. Speaking from personal experience, there is no more damaging combination than two sex addicts acting out toward each other, and nothing is more dangerous than when it happens at work.

> **"It's all about female submission: 'You're my ho. Get down on your knees.' When he finally got a girlfriend in high school, 'she pretty much became like garbage to me. I was always demanding more, putting my hands in the wrong places. I acted like her body was mine and I could do what I wanted.'"**
>
> *Another comment from Troy, 25-year-old college student. "The Cyberporn Generation," People, April 26, 2004.*

Going Underground

I mentioned before how college students live in a world of absolute tolerance when it comes to their sexual proclivities, and how most don't foresee the kinds of adjustments they'll need to make when entering the postcollege workforce. Yet even in their sexually permissive world they still find reasons to hide certain behaviors that even they would consider generally unacceptable to others. For instance, when asked, "Do you hide some of your sexual behavior from others?" a whopping 58% of the college men and 52% of the college women said "yes." We then asked a related question, "Have you ever worried about people finding out about your sexual activities?" Again, over half of the men, 53%, and exactly half of the women, 50%, said "yes."

Hiding our sexual behaviors from others because we're either too embarrassed or feel too guilty to face up to them sets a bad precedent, especially if our admission means we've been unfaithful to our mate or violated the rights of others at home or in the workplace. While this embarrassment might seem somewhat normal to some, it creates ideal conditions for feelings of guilt and shame and self-hatred to take root. Having nothing to hide from others about who you are and what you do is clearly preferable to always having something to hide.

When we asked students, "Do you ever feel bad about your sexual behavior?" 44% of the men and 39% of the women said "yes." Given the anything-goes mentality of today's campus culture, this high a percentage of students admitting that they feel bad about their sexual behavior surprised me. In yet another question directed at measuring sexual shame, we asked the students, "Have you ever felt degraded by your sexual behavior?" Here, a somewhat larger percentage of women than men said "yes"—33% compared to 29%. Still, roughly a third of all college students have felt degraded by their own sexual actions. In fact, about 12% of all college students (12% of the women and 11% of the men) even reported that they typically feel depressed after having sex.

Without a doubt, these students already have lots of experience hiding their sexual behavior due to feelings of guilt and shame, even in a relatively permissive campus environment. But what happens when they move from a campus to an office? If they're like many newly graduated employees, they'll make use of the skills they've developed over several years in college to conceal the sexual activities they feel compelled to engage in during the workday.

Losing Control

Americans have always had an interesting relationship with the word *control*. We seek to possess it, but fear losing it once we have it. Whether it's being "in control" of our own destinies, or "taking control" of our lives, being in some state of control is something we all want. Especially in our jobs, employers expect a high degree of maturity and self-control from their employees. But when it comes to sexual self-control, many college students admittedly struggle. When asked just how much control they feel they have over their sexual urges and desires, a key indicator of sexual compulsivity and addiction, the picture they paint for us is alarming.

One in 4 college men (26%) and nearly 1 in 5 in five college women (18%) said they have trouble stopping their sexual behavior when they know it's inappropriate. Their responses aren't just hypothetical; they're based on firsthand experience. This data should make every manager's and HR professional's pulse race. When it comes to inappropriate sexual behavior in the workplace, this is a recipe for disaster! As we all know, there is no room for half-measures here. If a certain sexual activity or behavior is prohibited as a rule of company policy (or by state or federal law), you just can't go there. But what if you have a hard time keeping those sexual fantasies and urges under control? In essence, that's what this group of students is telling us—that even in the face of potential consequences and serious reprimands for sexual behavior they know is inappropriate, many of them are losing those battles.

In fact, 38% of college men and 23% of college women go on to admit that they've actually tried to quit an unwanted sexual behavior and failed. Twenty-nine percent of women and 27% of men said they have times when they act out sexually followed by periods of celibacy, another clear sign of trying to quit. About 1 in 5 men (19%) and 1 in 10 women (10%) acknowledged that they actually feel controlled by their sexual desire or fantasies of romance. In fact, 1 in 4 men (26%) and 1 in 7 women (15%) have even thought that their sexual desires are stronger than they are. These feelings are common among the sexually addicted, which suggests that many of these students could be at significant risk of developing an addiction. So there is good reason for future employers to have cause for concern about the psychological and emotional readiness of many of today's graduates.

One of the most telling signs of the internal conflict raging within many students was their responses to the question, "Do you feel that your sexual behavior is not normal?" Again, 1 in 5 college men (21%) and a slightly smaller percentage of college women (15%) said that they feel that their sexual behavior is *not* normal. What's really interesting about this question is that the survey never attempts to define for them what is normal or abnormal sexual behavior. They answered based on what *they* consider to be normal sexual behavior, according to *their own* definition.

Yet in spite of these many signs of problematic sexual behaviors and related issues with guilt, shame, and self-control, only 9% of college men and 4% of college women have ever sought help for sexual behavior they did not like. Overall, just 7% of all of the college students we surveyed are asking for help for problematic sexual behavior.

Implications of the Survey

When analyzing all of the data from our online sex survey, it turns out that only about 1% of the students we surveyed had scores that would place them in the "high-risk" group for being sexually addicted now or developing sexually compulsive or addictive behaviors in the near future. But 22% overall fell into the "at-risk" group, meaning they are walking close to the boundary line of addiction. When compared to estimates that 6%–8% of the adult population in this country is sexually addicted, that's a large number of "at-risk" men and women.

Not surprisingly, men outnumbered women in both the at-risk and high-risk groups by a combined ratio of more than 2 to 1. Looking at only those students scoring above the median of 14 "yes" answers, men as a percentage made up over two-thirds of those who are more likely to become sexually compulsive and addictive later in life. While the consumption of pornography and the sexualization of the culture is increasingly becoming a women's issue, the porn industry and those who use sex to sell their products still cater mainly to men as their targeted and most cherished consumers. As a result, males in the workplace will continue to be the ones who most visibly struggle with adhering to company policies restricting or prohibiting certain sexual behaviors and acceptable Internet-use policies.

Few people would deny that the increased availability and mainstreaming of pornography has led to the normalization of pornographic attitudes, beliefs, and behaviors throughout a large part of society that were once considered unacceptable. As porn has become the norm, nowhere is that more evident than in the protected and sexualized environs of our college campuses. Within the confines of this cocooned subculture, every conceivable form and genre of sexuality is embraced under the banner of personal freedom and tolerance. Combine this with college students' easy access to a high-speed, wireless Internet environment that's usually unregulated, uncensored, and unmonitored—the antithesis of what you find in a typical business environment—and you've got a perfect breeding ground for unrealistic, and potentially harmful, sexual attitudes, beliefs, and behaviors. Many of these hypersexualized students will find accessing porn at work nearly impossible to resist—in spite of the potential consequences.

Of course, this raises a question that no business can ignore—what's going to happen when these two worlds collide?

Part 3

Finding a Better
Way to Work

WHEN WORLDS COLLIDE

In every good story, there is always a buildup of unresolved conflict, usually involving the main characters, that invariably leads to the climax or defining moment of the story that resolves the conflict. If we imagine this book in the context of a story—and in many ways it is no more than a collective story involving all of us—we have reached that place in the story where the tension is sure to rise. It's what always happens when characters from two very different worlds collide. The Have's meet the Have Not's. The Good Girl meets the Rebel. The Hillbillies move to Beverly Hills. And while our story involves many more characters than just those recent and upcoming Millennial grads I chose to highlight in the previous section, the stage couldn't be set any better for a classic confrontation.

- More than 70% of men between the ages of 18 and 34 visit a pornographic Web site in a typical month.

- 44% of U.S. workers with an Internet connection admitted to accessing an X-rated Web site at work in the month of March 2004, as compared to 40% of home users and 59% of university users.

Why do I say that? Well, on the one hand, you have the hyper-competitive world of the average American business. Whether large or small, local or international, today's business owners and managers have never before faced so many challenges in the midst of so great an opportunity to grow and prosper. In spite of all the negative news that tends to dominate our airwaves, businesses and business owners of all types and sizes can now enter a global marketplace with relative ease. Many can attract the capital needed to fuel their growth from organizations and individuals well beyond our borders.

Yet, to remain competitive and continue to grow requires sound strategies and determination. Today's global markets are far less forgiving than in the past, and the competition for limited supplies and resources can be fierce. The same holds true for sourcing human capital and labor. At a time when the world is getting flatter and increased access to global labor markets keeps changing the rules of the game, the winners are often those organizations that can increase their employees' productivity at lower costs than their competitors. Thus, every hiring decision is critical.

Enter the expansive labor pool of Millennials graduating from college and joining the job market. They're well educated, multitalented, and eager to begin their careers and make a difference in the world. They're tech savvy and heavily networked with their peers. For those mature enough, their future could indeed be bright, both theirs and their employers'.

Except for one small problem. A sizable percentage of them, especially the men, are bringing a nasty habit with them to work that they may or may not be able to just stop on their own: surfing for and downloading porn (and a lot of it); chat room conversations and text message exchanges loaded with overt sexual dialogue; and even some homemade, spur-of-the-moment porn—self-portraits sent from cell phone to cell phone, just for kicks. But it's more than just some bad habits by a few bad apples. It's the dominant mind-set, the preexisting sexual attitudes of an entire generation that are coming with them to work every day. Their sexual attitudes and beliefs have influenced the kind of behaviors that many in the business world would rather not even know about. That is, if it didn't represent such a serious risk and threat to their business.

But it does. Everyone in business management has heard the nightmarish stories and read the blazing headlines. They've thought about the kind of public embarrassment and close scrutiny their organizations would come under if it ever "happened to them." Sex scandal. Sexual harassment. Hostile workplace. Just the potential threat of a multimillion-dollar lawsuit is enough for many managers and business owners to say, "Go ahead and throw out the bathwater, the baby, and all the toys so that will never happen to us!" So the lines are drawn—zero tolerance. Or if they're feeling particularly sympathetic, maybe allow for a warning or two. But that's it. Repeat offenders are out the door, no questions asked. "We just can't take any chances."

Phil's Dilemma

Let's look at Phil, for example. Phil is a recent graduate of Porn University and a new employee. On his first day at work, Phil is handed the firm's Internet Acceptable Use Policy by the HR manager during a new employee orientation briefing. In it he reads, "No surfing for pornography, exchanging lewd photos, or sending obscene jokes or any other sexual content to anyone via the company's email system. No storing pornographic images on your business computer. Do not bring your personal laptop to work and plug it into the company network if it has even a trace of porn on it"—or something to that effect.

Now Phil's eyes are about as big as silver dollars. He doesn't get it—why the big deal about porn? After all, back on campus, the 'Net was wide-open, no blockers or filters of any kind. The only time the administration got even a little peeved was when they discovered that Phil's friend Jack had a three terabyte porn server stashed away in his dorm room closet that ate up the better part of the school's excess bandwidth as he fed pornographic images and pirated adult movies on demand to the rest of the student body via a popular peer-to-peer network service. Phil and all of his friends thought it was pretty funny, harmless stuff at the time.

But now, in an effort to comply and not get fired in his first week on the job, Phil offloads the porn on his notebook computer to an external drive so he won't get into trouble if he should ever need to bring his computer to work. He also signs the papers HR handed him, including that Internet AUP, where he promises not to look at porn or abuse the Internet (or fellow employees) while at work. That seemed simple enough.

However, Phil soon starts to discover that after spending a lifetime looking at porn, including a few hours a week those last five years in college, stopping that bad behavior on demand might not be so easy. He thinks, "Thank goodness I can still go home at night to my laptop and look at whatever I want to," as he realizes the new rules mean no surfing porn sites over lunch to break up the monotony and stress in his life.

Then, a few years later, he loses that safe haven, too, after meeting and marrying the woman of his dreams. A wonderful woman who, unlike some of the girls he met in college, is just as intolerant of his use of porn as his employer is.

So now, Phil really has no choice but to stop—assuming he can. If he can't, or more likely if he won't because he doesn't want to give up one of his favorite pastimes, then Phil will do what millions of others before him have done—keep his porn and sexual acting out habits intact but simply drive them further underground, hidden out of sight from everyone in his life. Phil knows a few others at work who have done the same thing. Some have gotten caught, but others haven't.

What's different for Phil and others of his generation is that they've been raised on perhaps the most explicit and habit-forming types of pornography known to man. So hiding his sexual behaviors and damping down his appetite for porn is going to be a real test of willpower. And if he's one of the unfortunate many who have already crossed the line into compulsive and addictive use of the material, this is a test he is bound to eventually fail. Maybe not tomorrow, or next month, or even next year. But by keeping these unwanted sexual behaviors hidden and simultaneously feeding them in secret, he's setting himself up for a certain fall. Yet, he sees no other option. No one talks about this topic in a way that he feels safe coming out and admitting that he's struggling and trying to quit. So he lives in denial of the severity of his growing problem and tries his best to manage the unmanageable.

From the company's standpoint, as long as Phil doesn't bring his bad habit into the workplace, they're happy. However, what they don't realize is that they have now become part of the problem by setting up rigid policies and reinforcing the existing social stigmas surrounding sexual addiction and compulsivity by not allowing or encouraging their employees like Phil to get the kind of help they need when they're ready to ask for it. I will elaborate on this in the next chapter, but dealing with this problem in a way that benefits both the company and the employee requires viewing it as a wellness issue, in much the same way that companies now deal with employees facing alcohol addiction or substance abuse.

Stories like Phil's are not really a new phenomenon or unique to the emergence of the Millennials in our modern-day workforce. It's been going on for years, even decades, this clashing of two worlds at work. What has changed is the potency of the material and its availability to employees at work. In fact, the very productivity tools that we celebrate and equip our workers with—the Internet, wireless communications, PDAs, 3G networks, collaborative technologies, and social networking—have become a staple of pornographers and the adult entertainment industry.

In fact, many of the technological breakthroughs in the world of e-commerce that we take for granted today, like streaming video and new ways to pay for content, were driven and even developed by the porn industry. So while it's true that new digital technologies bring many good things to life, they also represent significant Pavlovian "triggers" to legions of users, young and old, who now struggle on a daily basis with Internet porn and sexually compulsive and addictive behaviors.

> **"'This dilemma is going to get much worse, given the capacity of handheld, electronic devices to download porn,' says Carleton Kendrick, a psychotherapist in Millis, MA. 'That will eliminate an employer's opportunity to check which workers have been going to porn sites on company computers.'"**
>
> Stephanie Armour, "Technology Makes Porn Easier to Access at Work," USA Today, October 17, 2007.

The Times They Are a-Changin'

The sociosexual situation is changing as it relates to our use and tolerance of pornography. While some are willing to recognize and accept the fact that psychological disorders like sexual addiction are in part driven by the easy availability and use of pornography, others deny these disorders exist and refuse to accept any cause-and-effect relationships. So while our society at large debates the issues in the midst of conflicting values, the sentiments of those in the business world are clear: porn and sexual misconduct have no place at work.

Personally, I couldn't agree more. Pornography and sexually explicit images, messages, or conversation have no place in the work environment and should not be tolerated. In fact, these are certainly justified as grounds for dismissal in the case of repeated violations by employees, managers, or anyone working on behalf of the organization. Violators expose the organization to a very real threat of sexual harassment and hostile workplace environment lawsuits, public embarrassment and ridicule, and harm done to other employees as well as customers, suppliers, and other business associates. Without a doubt, in the ultracompetitive world of business, porn is a serious matter and its presence should not be tolerated.

However, here's the dilemma we face. *We*—the American business sector—helped to create this beast, and for the most part we're now turning our backs on its victims as well as its misguided fans. As the adult entertainment industry grew, we protected it with our laws and helped to legitimize it by inviting its companies to go public and sell stock. We stood by as hotel owners and hotel chain conglomerates started piping porn into their guest rooms, and hardly paid attention as they even became collaborators with big porn by boldly advertising to their guests that they would hide the titles of any adult movies they bought when printing up their final bill. We defended the rights of pornographers to print and publish their material so they could freely distribute it to consumers everywhere. And when those consumers started showing up on the Web, we once again embraced the porn industry's e-commerce business models and started becoming more pornographic ourselves in marketing and advertising our goods and services on the Internet. After all, everyone knows that sex sells.

Winning Hearts and Minds through Porn

When you consider how powerful and dominant the American free enterprise system has been throughout the past hundred years, it should come as no surprise that in our efforts to legitimize and help the porn industry in America grow, it has done so quite brilliantly. While the form and format of the material has changed over time, there's no doubt that America remains the world's largest producer and exporter of pornographic material.

> **"Sensing the start of a profitable new era for pocket porn, the adult entertainment industry is investing heavily and feverishly broadening its marketplace of iPhone porn. . . . Leading porn purveyors see the iPhone as a dream come true."**
>
> Jeremy Caplan, "The iPhone's Next Frontier: Porn," Time, June 18, 2008

The only place where we have lost our former leadership position is as the world's biggest consumers of porn. Not that the number of porn consumers in the U.S. has declined, we've just done such a great job of exporting our pornographic material that the rest of the world is catching up and starting to look more like us. At the same time Western values projected through pornography, like the objectification and sexualization of women and men, have been a big export of ours into other cultures around the world. Even in our own homegrown cubicles great cultural collisions are taking place between people like Phil and his employer.

So when we take a good look at employees like Phil, we might be wise to consider what kind of product our pornographic culture has created before we decide to let them go and "pass the trash" to the next employer (as this practice is so affectionately referred to in our educational system) once we discover that they're struggling with sex and porn. Because for every employee who surfaces and is exposed as a violator of our sexually related company policies and Internet AUPs, I can assure you that there are ten others hiding in our hallways and operating under the radar yet to be discovered. The price we pay for creating this hostile environment of fear and condemnation could very well lead to every CEO's worst nightmare becoming a reality.

The "L" Word—
WHAT KEEPS CEOs
UP *at* NIGHT

If you're a CEO or key leader or stakeholder in any business or organization, reading the headlines and the accompanying news blurbs in the preface of this book probably quickened your pulse a bit. Interspersed among those headlines were stories that make most CEOs I know lose sleep at night.

The very idea of having an employee's sexual indiscretions making headlines in some newspaper or popular business magazine is cause enough for concern. But when you consider the ramifications of a well-publicized, multimillion dollar sexual harassment or hostile workplace environment lawsuit brought against your organization by an employee or

- Nearly one-third of U.S. Fortune 500 companies have had sexual harassment cases filed against them by employees objecting to their colleagues' Internet viewing habits.

- More than 30% of 1,500 surveyed companies have terminated employees for inappropriate use of the Internet, while only 37.5% of companies use filtering software.

- In 2003 employees at the UK Dept of Work and Pensions downloaded some two million pages of pornographic content. Of these two million some 1800 contained child pornography.

business associate—well, I don't know many leaders who sleep well at night in the midst of defending themselves and their organization in such circumstances.

"In one case, the EEOC alleged that First Mutual, a mortgage company in Cherry Hill, N.J., subjected a male employee to a sexually hostile work environment, sexual harassment by a female co-worker and retaliatory firing when he complained. According to the lawsuit, the alleged harasser e-mailed nude photos of herself and of another woman to the man's company computer. A First Mutual spokesman, saying the case had been settled, declined to comment."

Stephanie Armour, "Technology Makes Porn Easier to Access at Work," USA Today, October 17, 2007.

Reading those stories may well bring a lump to your throat as you ask yourself, "What would we do? How would we survive the fallout? Are we doing enough now to prevent something like that from ever happening to *us?*" While it would be easy to write an entire book on this complex subject alone, I'm going to focus on a brief overview of the kind of litigation risks you could be facing with a workforce experiencing everything from mild sex syndrome to full-fledged sexual addictions, and more importantly, what you should be doing today to best mitigate those risks.

The Changing Face of Legal Liability

If only one news story in the preface grabbed your attention, I hope it was the first story from Human Resource Executive Online entitled, "Internet Addiction: The Next Disability?" The case involved an IBM employee who sued for wrongful termination after he was fired for using his work computer to visit an Internet sex chat room. He claimed protection under the Americans with Disabilities Act in his lawsuit against IBM for $5 million, saying he suffered from an addiction to pornography that was triggered by post-traumatic stress disorder arising from his service in the Vietnam War. The story's author, an expert in the area of human resources management, commented, "Although the employee's argument that he suffers from an addiction to online pornography and is thus eligible for protection under the Americans with Disabilities Act may not stand up in court, others—including the authors of a recent university study—say that Internet addiction is indeed real. . . . Companies may find themselves liable for their employees' porn-related Web-surfing if they fail to take action."[1]

In the midst of the growing debate over whether Internet porn addiction (what could be labeled a subset of sexual addiction) is a legitimate illness like alcoholism, recognition by a court that it is an uncontrollable addiction, and not just a bad habit, could redefine the condition as a psychological impairment worthy of protection under the Americans with Disabilities Act (ADA). That would have far-reaching ramifications for how companies deal with workplace Internet use and the consumption of porn at work. For one thing, businesses might then have to provide medical leave, counseling, or make some other accommodation for employees who struggle at work with the urge to surf Internet porn sites due to their addiction.

Brian East, cochair of the disability rights committee of the National Employment Lawyers' Association, says recognizing Internet abuse as an addiction would make it more difficult for employers to fire employees who have a problem. "Assuming it is recognized as an impairment . . . it is analyzed the same way as alcoholism," says East.[2]

Of course, that's a significant assumption. Although the American Psychiatric Association (APA) doesn't include sexual or Internet porn addictions in the *Diagnostic and Statistical Manual of Mental Disorders* the way it lists alcohol dependency as an addiction, it does include substance abuse. Most employee health-care plans and EAPs (Employee Assistance Programs) provide services for those suffering from both alcoholism and substance abuse, but not for Internet porn or sexual addiction. Either of those will not be eligible for inclusion in the manual until around 2012, when the next edition is scheduled to be released, according to the APA. Whatever the APA's stance might be, more and more psychiatrists and psychologists are affirming that compulsive Internet use, for whatever purpose, can legitimately be called an addiction and are treating patients for that condition—albeit at a higher cost to patients, who have to foot the entire bill on their own.

Then there's the case of the New Jersey Court of Appeals who held on the eve of 2006 that employers have a duty to uncover and stop an employee's use of corporate electronic resources for child porn activities once the employer knows, or should know, that an employee has accessed adult pornography. Doe *v.* XYC Corp. provides a whole new basis of employment litigation that seeks to hold employers responsible for the damages to victims of crimes committed by employees using corporate electronic resources.[3]

While I realize there will always be some frivolous lawsuits mixed in with legitimate ones related to this issue, the bigger picture here is that there are now even more reasons for employers to take these matters seriously and become more proactive in addressing them. Although an increased threat of lawsuits looms in the not-too-distant future as a growing number of employees try to overcome sexual addiction on their own, there is a way to lower your risk of getting sued while at the same time helping your employees who are struggling get the help they need to get well. But before I explain how, I'd like to first comment on what I see as the predominant approaches being taken by most businesses today to try to manage employees' use and abuse of technology in regard to sexual misbehavior.

The Right Approach: Discipline or Treatment?

When it comes to dealing with employees who abuse the Internet or office equipment and systems for sexual purposes, most companies I know take a disciplinarian approach to addressing this problematic behavior. If an employee violates the policy, then warnings, discipline, and termination may follow.

According to a 2006 study conducted by the American Management Association, 51% of the businesses surveyed said they had disciplined employees for misusing the Internet, while 26% had even fired workers for it.[4] This approach has many adherents, including a growing number of organizations that have also taken the extreme stance of removing the warnings and reprimands and have adopted a "zero-tolerance" policy of immediate termination.

> "It's not as easy as transferring a Casanova to a different department— although transferring him to a different continent might solve the problem for a while. That's how the Fortune 500 have frequently handled these kinds of problems in the past."
>
> Betsy Morris, "Addicted to Sex," Fortune, May 10, 1999.

While this may seem like an attractive stance to some, I see several problems with it. For one, the clear message to employees seems to be "If you've got a problem with this, better handle it on your own because we sure won't help you." For those like me whose battle with Internet porn grew over many years before I actually became addicted, our reaction will be to go further underground with our behaviors. Of course, as I stated earlier in the book, hiding the problem simply reinforces the feelings of guilt and shame we experience over what we do in secret. Since guilt and shame are the primary fuels that propel the addictive cycle, our sexual compulsivity and addictive behaviors will almost always grow worse over time—usually until we get caught. At some point, the threats of reprimand or even dismissal might not be enough to cause us to stop, since after we've crossed a certain point we really can't stop—at least not on our own.

The other extreme result that can come from the disciplinarian approach is what I refer to as "passing the trash." Actually, I didn't invent that term. I first saw it used in an article I read that told of how certain school districts, when faced with a "problem teacher," would pass that teacher on to some other school district where he would become their problem. "Out of sight, out of mind" might be a better description. Either way, everyone loses in the end because by "passing the trash"—the person with the problem who can't stop his behavior on his own—you only make the problem worse for that person, his family, and his next employer. And while that strategy may seem to be the easiest and safest way for that employee's supervisor to respond, who's to say that this fired employee won't pop up again working for someone else in your company's supply chain or for a valued customer and cause you even more headaches?

A milder form of the disciplinarian approach involves focusing on the person's behavior as a performance issue instead of considering that there may be underlying issues driving his violating behaviors and working with him to help uncover what they are so he can deal with them. In areas like this where the difficulties at work might stem from emotional or psychological problems, enlisting the help of an EAP counselor or psychologist can be a catalyst for change as a first step toward healing. Of course, most programs today don't recognize disorders like sexual compulsivity or sexual addiction as legitimate psychological illnesses. That is all the more reason why many in the business world resort to the disciplinarian approach when it comes to handling these kinds of sexual misconduct work issues.

The other approach is what I'll call the treatment approach. Instead of viewing the employee as a "bad person" in need of discipline and insisting on varying levels of close supervision bordering on unlawful invasions of privacy, the treatment approach grants the individual the same level of respect as any other employee in need of health care or medical assistance. The goal is to create a safe environment at work whereby employees who struggle in this area are encouraged to seek out help long before their unwanted sex-ual behavior becomes a compulsive addiction. Awareness training and employee education can be a key component to helping them recognize what the warning signs are for Internet porn and sexual addiction—whether it's their own addiction or something they see in a co-worker whose sexual acting out behaviors are affecting the work environment.

If your current EAP provider doesn't offer qualified counseling and assistance in this area, shop around for one who does or counselors who are willing to serve the needs of your organization in this area on a supplemental basis. While it may cost your business extra to make such an arrangement, if it helps one employee keep it together and learn to overcome this lifelong struggle by deal-ing with it instead of continuing to deny the problem, it will have been worth the investment.

> **"'This issue is huge. It's becoming a bigger and bigger problem,' says Richard Chaifetz, CEO of ComPsych, a Chicago-based employee assistance provider."**
>
> Stephanie Armour, "Technology Makes Porn Easier to Access at Work," USA Today, October 17, 2007.

Of course, there will be some employees who need help but aren't ready and willing to recognize that they've got a serious problem. In that case, and in my opinion all cases involving potential sexual addiction, what is needed is a "three-strikes" or comparable disci-plinary policy, but one that invites and encourages the employee to utilize recovery resources for hope and help.

The key is to lead with a compassionate approach of respecting the individual as a person in need of help, and being willing to part-ner with him in getting the kind of help he needs before considering harsher disciplinary measures. While the employee is seeking out help or going through the process of recovery, it's not unreason-able to expect him to abide by the same acceptable use policies that apply to everyone else. However, in the early stages of recovery, part of the healing process may require that the individual severely limit or cut off access to the Internet altogether both at work and at home. For that reason, certain adjustments in how that employee does his work might need to be made. In the case of someone whose job requires that he use a networked computer most if not all of the time (e.g., a network systems administrator or technical support person), he may soon discover in recovery that he needs to change jobs or careers, at least for a while, in order to get well. Still, it's better to find that out early on in the recovery process than allow the person to continue to struggle and hide until something major blows up at work or in his personal life. True addiction recovery is anything but an easy out for addicts. Entering recovery is the toughest choice they'll ever have to make, but for most it's the only one that will truly help set them free.

Another factor that will be absolutely critical for that employee's success in recovery and in his ability to improve his performance at work is being held accountable by his manager and a peer for his actions at work and at home. This is a built-in part of any 12-step program (several reputable 12-step groups are listed in the appendixes of this book). Anyone who says he's in recovery but isn't accountable to at least one specific, named person other than a spouse or significant other is not really in recovery. Especially for those employees who operate mostly on their own and/or travel regularly as a part of their jobs, I recommend they have at least three accountability partners who receive regular computer log summary reports of every Web site they visit on at least a weekly basis.

Several excellent Internet accountability products are available out there that do just that for a couple of bucks per person per month, without putting an extra burden on your IT department, such as Covenant Eyes and BSafe Online. In fact, I personally believe that every employee and manager who works mostly on their own should be encouraged to have an accountability partner and utilize such tools as an added reminder to help them make wise choices on how they spend their time both online and away from the computer.

When it comes to the employee who is in recovery, being account-able to others on a daily basis for his actions should not be an option. If he resists or refuses to do so, then he isn't really ready to give up his drug of choice and stricter disciplinary measures should be taken, including, if necessary, dismissal from his job. It's that important, and every former addict who's been through recovery knows it.

From Reactive to Proactive

Growing up in an athletic family, sports and competition became a metaphor for everything we did. In the case of a business or or-ganization trying to avoid ending up in court and in the headlines over an embarrassing sex scandal or sexual misdeed by one of its employees, the best defense is . . . well, a good offense! An offensive strategy, that is.

One key to limiting your liability in lawsuits stemming from the sexual misbehavior of an employee is to take the offensive and com-mit to educating and training your employees on the dangers of In-ternet and porn addictions. This also opens the topic up for public discussion, and helps relieve the perceived stigma in the minds of all employees. It's also absolutely essential that you be ready to offer real help to those who will recognize, as a result of the training, that they are the ones who are struggling.

Sitting back in a defensive posture with a disciplinarian's rod in hand and waiting for those who violate your rules and policies to pop up so you can fire them and "pass the trash" on to someone else is NOT the way to solve this problem. Whether that's your true intent or not is immaterial—it's how your employees and managers perceive your position on such issues that really counts. If those who struggle in secret think that it will be safe to step forward and ask for help, I believe that in time they will. I would have. But first you have to create that safe environment and make sure that everyone in your company knows you're sincere and serious about wanting to help those who struggle. Until that happens, whether you realize it or not, you're already creating a hostile work environment for addicts and potential victims alike. But there is a better way.

Sometimes the best way to solve a complex problem is to start with a change of heart

THE FIRST STEP *to* SOLVING *a* COMPLEX PROBLEM

The issues surrounding addiction that I've outlined in the preceding chapters are certainly more complex than any single book can address. Human beings are inherently complex, and complicated, and capable of great insight and wisdom—but also of great irrationality and self-destruction. We can create incredible messes and yet leave others in awe at our ability to fix things and make them right. We are demolition and restoration experts all

• Half of the Fortune 500 companies have dealt with at least one incident related to computer porn over a twelve-month period. Offenders were fired in 44% of the incidents and disciplined in a further 41% of cases. (Reported July 2005)

• Of 61 million unique U.S. visitors logged into pornographic Web sites in March of 2006, every fifth visitor was from an office workstation.

rolled into one. Where some only see the drawbacks of our personalities, others see us shine in our brilliance. That is why people will always be our greatest assets and biggest competitive advantages, yet at the same time, they will represent our biggest liabilities. So when it comes to adding our sexuality into the mix of our work lives, it's no surprise that many of us who work with and manage employees are uneasy about the subject matter I've been talking about in this book. There are things we'd just rather tell our employees to leave at home, asking them in essence to separate who they are from what we pay them to do. But, once again, it's more complicated than that.

What's most amazing to me about all of this, especially knowing full well as I write this book how incredibly complex these issues and problems can be, is how uniquely simple the first step to solving the problem can be.

"I wish my husband was an alcoholic or a drug addict instead," one desperate spouse of a sex addict confided to me over the phone just days after her husband was hospitalized for attempting suicide. He had become distraught over his losing battle with sexual addiction and felt hopeless. So earlier that week, with his wife and children standing near him on a sidewalk, he stepped out into the path of a speeding car in a failed attempt to end it all. This husband and father is a well respected and high profile county official who had been struggling with his sexual addiction for years with no help offered by his employer.

> "'Most of my patients are CEOs or doctors or attorneys or priests,' says Patrick J. Carnes. (Author's note: Dr. Carnes is the nation's leading expert on sexual addiction and director of the Gentle Path program for sexual addiction recovery.) 'They are people with a great deal of power. We have corporate America's leadership marching through here, and they're paying cash because they don't want anybody to know.'"
>
> Betsy Morris, "Addicted to Sex," Fortune, May 10, 1999.

"The few people around him who knew about it were in a state of denial themselves, just hoping he could fix this problem on his own or that it would somehow just go away," she later explained. "We have the best health care coverage through the county government he works for that anyone could ever want, and they said if he was an alcoholic or had a substance abuse problem, they'd pay for everything he needed, including an expensive inpatient treatment program. But they won't pay a dime to help him with his sexual addiction. They told us we're on our own, and the people at one of the few reputable inpatient sexual addiction recovery clinics that I spoke with told me I'd need to pay them $50,000 just to get in the door! Who can afford that?!"

Later on in my conversation with her, this distressed spouse started wondering whether she should take out a second mortgage on their home to pay for her husband's care. "I don't know what to do," she said, on the verge of tears. "He wants to deal with this but knows he needs help. So what do we do now?"

To be honest, I wasn't really sure what to tell her at the time. Before I got off the phone, I offered to talk with him and get more involved in personally helping them to get the help they needed. Eventually, I did help them come up with an aggressive plan for recovery that they could afford. I pray for that family and many others like them because sometimes it's all you can do for those trying to get help and find hope in the face of an unfair burden of society-wide denial that our struggles even exist. And that's not right! Not in this country, this Porn Nation, where we allow good people to be sexually exploited for the sake of the almighty dollar and through the mechanism of our free enterprise system, only to shut the door on those who have bought into our media messages and pornographic come-ons and consumed too much. They deserve better, and we owe it to them to wake up to the reality that we created and fed this beast all these years, and now it's time that we all accept some responsibility for helping them learn to tame it and even eradicate it from their lives.

The First Step: Equal Access EAP

Without a doubt, these are complex problems and issues we're dealing with. But there is a first step toward a practical solution. It is a positive first step, an "about-face" and change in direction from the no-win path we are on now to one that restores hope and offers help to millions of people and their families who are struggling and suffering in silence.

That first step: offer sex addicts and those who struggle equal access to the help and services they need through employee assistance programs (EAPs). In other words, provide the same health care benefits to employees (and their dependents on eligible plans) who struggle with sexual compulsivity and addiction as you would to any other employee suffering from addictive disorders like alcoholism or drug dependence. That's it. Equal access. Not that complicated and not that costly when you compare it to the cost of continuing to do nothing in the midst of a growing epidemic of sexually related lawsuits and productivity losses. Because more than anything, it's a change in attitude.

We've been here before, you know. There was a day in this country when alcoholism and drug addiction were viewed by both medical experts and psychologists as mainly the result of a lack of character or weaknesses in willpower and self-control. Alcoholics were considered bums and the dregs of society, most often seen disheveled and literally lying in the gutter. Cast in the same light as the homeless, decades went by in our country before we started noticing that not all alcoholics were lying in the gutter. Most, in fact, wore a suit and tie and went to work in offices all across the country. Many others were at home raising families and driving kids to school and the ballpark.

That was life in America in the '50s and '60s, around the time we started waking up as a nation to the reality that alcoholics and alcoholism permeated every occupation and every socioeconomic strata of society. This change in perspective was due in large part to a grassroots level movement that began back in 1939 called Alcoholics Anonymous (AA). This fellowship of struggling and suffering alcoholics decided not to wait around for the medical establishment to do something about a very real health epidemic that was sweeping the nation and affecting millions of families. Thanks to the collective determination and courage of these ad-hoc healing communities, needed changes have taken place in our country to bring real hope and help to millions of suffering alcoholics and their families who choose to get well.

But it took a long time for our society as a whole to come around, set our prejudices aside, and finally recognize and accept the fact that alcoholism is a very real and treatable condition. Eventually, businesses, insurance companies, and yes, even the medical establishment woke up and started becoming part of the solution instead of being part of the problem.

Unbeknownst to most people, one group that plays a pivotal role in whether or not millions of Americans get the mental health care they need is a highly politicized group called the American Psychiatric Association, or APA. As authors and publishers of the *Diagnostic and Statistical Manual of Mental Disorders* (or DSM-IV, for fourth edition), they are the gatekeepers of what psychiatric conditions will and won't qualify for coverage under most health care benefit plans. In short, the DSM is the official map of mental illnesses and disorders in the United States. Sadly, in the world of psychiatrists and insurers, if your disorder is not on the map, then it doesn't exist.

While it took a long time for the medical community to come around and recognize alcoholism as a bona-fide form of mental illness (it was first mentioned in the DSM-I published in 1952), it's taken even longer for the business community and the rest of society to accept the fact that alcoholics are people, too, worthy of our respect and deserving of the very best that our health care community has to offer.

We now find ourselves facing a similar situation with sexual addiction as we once did back in the '50s and '60s with alcoholism—

the same social stigmas, ignorance, ridicule, and condemnation, not to mention the same unwillingness by businesses, insurance companies, and health care providers to deal with this growing epidemic. While many will continue to think that if they just ignore the problem it will go away on its own, we've already learned from the lessons of the past that problems like sexual addiction rarely just go away. And the price we pay for our ignorance can be immeasurable.

The Greatest Businessman Who Never Was

Earlier in this book, I shared my personal story of a twenty-year business career spent mostly in denial of a serious problem that started out with viewing pornography and evolved over time into a full-blown sexual addiction. That addiction left undealt with eventually cost me everything. Even more painful, however, was the way my growing addiction stole my future hopes and dreams, leaving me to look back on my life wondering what could have been. From a work and career perspective, it's the story of the greatest salesman who never was. But I am not alone in that story.

For a long time, while growing up as the youngest in a family of five, I looked up to my father and was absolutely convinced that he was the greatest businessman who ever lived. My father was a company man, spending nearly his entire adult life working for just one company—the Jos. T. Ryerson and Sons steel company. My dad loved that company and his job and moved up in the ranks from inside sales in Chicago to the general manager of the Spokane, Washington, office, the smallest in a nationwide network of steel distribution centers. Like most company men of his era (my dad started his twenty-nine-year career with Ryerson back in 1952), he was fiercely loyal to his employer, worked countless hours on the job, and aspired to one day be president of the company. As he was promoted and moved into new locations and positions of greater responsibility over the years, this tireless promoter of the American free enterprise system appeared well on his way to achieving his greatest hopes and dreams. But there was just one problem. As a rising star in management in one of the classic industrial sectors, he was expected to entertain customers and suppliers with a constant flow of cocktail parties and booze-laden conventions. And my dad was an alcoholic.

He wasn't born that way, mind you. But close. Growing up in Chicago as the youngest in a family of nine, including seven athletic Irish boys, most of his brothers and their friends drank. He was able to hold back on drinking, heeding a special request his mother made of him, until going off to serve in the military during World War II. After the war ended, he joined what seemed like the rest of society in the accepted practice of keeping a cigarette in one hand and a drink in the other. Society not only expected it, but seemed to embrace it for decades before we started learning the truth about the health problems brought on by smoking and drinking. By then, my dad was in too deep to quit. And since it had practically become a job requirement for aspiring managers to throw caution to the wind and entertain clients with booze, he never seemed very motivated to give up either one.

When I first started to notice my dad's drinking problem, I was too young to understand why he would get so mad at me, enraged at times beyond what seemed to be justifiable anger. Of course, like most young kids growing up around the intermittent rages of an addict of any kind, I took it personally and started to think of myself as a bad kid, even defective in some ways. But as I got older and saw what everyone else saw but no one wanted to deal with or talk about, I rebelled. I'm sure that added to the pressure that my dad felt at work and dealing with the rest of us kids. Regardless of the fact that I always admired my dad's charismatic personality and strength of character, this was a character flaw I didn't have a lot of respect for—especially since he lived in a constant state of denial that he ever had a drinking problem. The rest of us, from my mom right down to me, became his enablers as he got older and weaker and became less of a source of tension and conflict in our lives.

My dad was certainly a brilliant businessman. However, a strategic move to Spokane to manage one of the company's smallest distribution facilities left him stuck in the backwoods of eastern Washington looking for a way to "get back to Chicago" and the company's home office, where the parking lot was dotted with reserved spaces for presidents and vice presidents. That was his dream, but his growing drinking problem always seemed to get in the way. Finally, as my mother describes, he started to abandon his lifelong dream of climbing the ranks to upper management because "he knew there would be a lot more entertaining at that level, and that meant drinking." In a strange twist of fate, one of the things that helped to elevate my dad's career—being the life of the party and great at entertaining customers and suppliers—was the very thing he feared in spite of his continued self-denial that his drinking had become a problem. So they stayed in Spokane until his retirement in 1981. Still, my dad could never hide the longing in his heart for the life that could have been.

Dad didn't try to stop smoking until around the time of his retirement. By then, the damage had already been done. Although my mom's health was solid as the Rock of Gibraltar, my dad's was anything but. While he eventually did quit smoking, for the most part he never did completely lay down the liquor until his mind was wracked with dementia and doctors finally forced him to just a few weeks before his death at the young age of seventy nine. The doctors had been treating him for a number of health conditions as he lay in a hospital room and then a nursing home bed in the final weeks of his life. One of those conditions was cirrhosis of the liver, and his doctors told him that due to the medications they had him on, his use of alcohol was strictly prohibited. I'm told his immediate response to them was, "Well, it's okay if I just have a small glass of wine, isn't it?" That statement more than anything sums up what I remember most about my dad's relationship with alcohol and how he lived as a prisoner to the ceaseless demands it put on his life and ours.

I wish I could say that my dad died peacefully, but he didn't. Not really, except for perhaps those final few minutes where I watched in amazement as his eyes locked onto my mom's, the love of his life, and without words it was clear that their shared love was as full of vitality as ever. My father was a good man, and he is missed dearly by all of us, but by no one more than my mother. It may be true that choices he made early in life cheated them both out of what could have been many more happy, healthy years together. We'll never know. But one thing I do know is that the way he lived and died serves as a stark reminder to us all of the ultimate price we pay for the choices we make along the way, and of what can happen when you live for so long in a state of denial that it blinds you from seeing the truth about who you are.

I believe that my dad did finally wake up to the truth, if only through very brief God-given glimpses of what could have been. I'll never forget the last words he ever spoke to me. In a moment of clarity that broke through his dementia-ridden mind, he looked me straight in the eyes and said, "It wasn't worth it."

My dad never offered any explanation of just what he meant— but I knew. I was the one who had challenged him the most about his drinking over the years, and this had sometimes strained our relationship. Even as we both got older and mellowed toward each other, I knew that he knew exactly how I felt whenever he held a glass of wine in his hand. Interestingly, my oldest sister, Cathy, recently shared with me for the first time the last words he spoke to her just the week before. "No more booze!" There's no question in my mind that with the end of his life now in sight, my dad finally got it. But the question is, will we? Or will we also live in denial until it's too late?

While it would be unfair to say that anyone other than my father was to blame for his addictions and not getting the help he needed when he needed it, it's also true that a lot of us stood around and did very little to help steer him onto a different path. Today, most employers would offer him an 800-number and a private consultation with a qualified counselor as a first step into recovery. There would be informational materials at work describing what to do if you or someone you love is showing the telltale signs of addiction. Maybe there would even be an attempt by his boss or friends or family at an intervention, where hurt feelings and bottom lines would be shared and treatment options would be offered.

Back then, in the early days of corporate personnel departments and long before the advent of seeing employees as "human resources," such care and concern for the whole individual didn't really exist the way it does now. But in this particular area of sexual compulsivity and addiction, are we really willing to roll up our sleeves and help our most valued assets grow and mature to the point where we help them slay the dragons that are consuming their lives, or have we reverted back to the days where employees are just expendable resources that can quickly and easily be replaced?

In those days, my father knew that coming forward and admitting to having a drinking problem, then asking the company for help to overcome it, was occupational suicide. So in those rare moments when he seemed more willing than not to seek out help, he opted not to in what appeared to him to be a black-and-white decision to survive and not jeopardize his livelihood and ours. But in failing to create a safe environment where one of their most productive and hardworking employees would be encouraged to overcome an unyielding disease called alcoholism, my father's employer settled instead for leaving him alone as a small-town manager with a drinking problem. If only they had known that by taking a slightly different tack, and helping him get well, they could have had one of the greatest businessmen who ever was. Will we make the same mistake they did?

CONCLUSION:

RESTORING RESPECT
for the INDIVIDUAL

Looking back over my business career, I think about the valuable lessons I learned along the way, going back to my early days at IBM. Of course, I didn't have a clue about what I was doing at the time. But I was fortunate to have been in one of the last groups of new hires to experience IBM's highly respected sales training program. It was eighteen grueling months of alternating classroom education and field training before earning the right to be called an IBM Account Executive. The reward was a new sales territory and a huge sales quota.

In many respects, they gave me the equivalent of a master's degree in business education that was far beyond anything I could have ever experienced attending any school. Although decades of real-world business experience has since added to my business acumen, there is one lesson I have never forgotten. I learned it on my first day of work: The first of IBM's three core beliefs—respect for the individual. This core belief always came

- In 1995, Chevron Corp. paid $2.2 million to settle a sexual harassment case brought by employees who were offended, in part, by an email titled "25 reasons beer is better than women."

- According to the report on Commercial Sexual Exploitation of Children in the U.S., 200,000 to 300,000 children are victims of commercial sexual exploitation in this country alone.

- Approximately 20% of all Internet pornography involves children.

before the other two and always garnered the most attention from management and those of us in the field. As a result, it served us well, bringing us all much success not just in our business dealings but also in everyday relationships—because after all, much like life itself, business is really all about relationships.

Today, though, I'm not so sure where "respect for the individual" stacks up compared with other themes that get played out in the busy world of commerce. Most of what we hear about today echoes the greed and financial ambitions of today's stakeholders with a very narrow focus on short-term profits. The problem is that people don't quite work like most other business assets, and getting a decent return on your investment in human capital can take some time. In addition, taking a good employee and turning him or her into a great employee takes management skill and a lot of patience, and sometimes a little good fortune as well. Yet the returns can be stellar, giving your business or organization a life of itself that will remain long after you leave the scene.

Of course, in order to reap those returns, we must discard our old ways of doing things and look at our organizations and the people we've entrusted with their care in new and

> **"Different companies have very different standards for what's considered inappropriate. 'We had a very senior salesperson who was a very bad actor' at IBM, recalls Kanin-Lovers (Jill Kanin-Lovers had top-level human resources jobs at IBM, American Express, and Towers Perrin before joining Avon Products). 'He was one of our best producers, but we fired him. There was no way we could allow him to go unpunished.' Still, she says, 'I grant you, you can go to other companies that will turn a blind eye if the guy is delivering results. You have companies that will say, "We care No. 1 about results, so we'll ignore these problems."'"**
>
> *Betsy Morris, "Addicted to Sex," Fortune, May 10, 1999.*

creative ways. One of those approaches is what I've recommended here—treating all employees equally, including those struggling with sexual compulsivity and addiction, and giving them equal access to the health benefits and EAPs you've put into place to help them live healthier, happier lives both at work and at home.

Though the corporate world often has difficulty seeing beyond the bottom line, respect for the individual is always the *right* approach. To put it bluntly, sex addicts are people too. They may not be the easiest to identify in your organization, and they may display some behaviors at work that leave people scratching their heads. But deep down, they want to get better. They *all* want to get better. Some, sadly, are lost in a fog of denial and will be too self-consumed and stubborn to ask for help or receive it when offered. For employees who are offered help when confronted but refuse, the best thing you can do for them is fire them. It's better to quicken their fall and bring them to the brokenness that awaits them at rock bottom than to ignore their plight or, even worse, become an enabler as an organization that continues to let them off the hook.

But for those who know they're sick and want to get well, we should be there for them with the resources that will help them get well. A caring attitude and an offer of professional help can be pivotal in giving your employees the courage they'll need to emerge from the dangerous shadow world they inhabit and set their feet on the road to recovery. Such assistance can also help turn your average to subpar performing employee into a passionate, stellar performer who will show fervent loyalty to the ones who helped to set them free from what for most has been a lifelong struggle.

Offering the Option of Faith-based Recovery

When it comes to recovery from sexual addiction, many people's pathway to redemption comes by way of both conventional and faith-based 12-step programs and counseling. In fact, when you take a closer look at the origins of the 12-step movement, you'll discover that faith played a major role going all the way back to the days of AA's founder, Bill Wilson. The group's insistence that participants deal with spiritual issues and recognize the existence of a "higher power" serves an important role in recovery. In my own experience, once I was willing to admit that I wasn't God and that I needed God's help in order to get well, important changes began to take place in my life. Changes that occurred from the inside out that eventually helped me heal and mend broken relationships. Changes that made me a better, more caring, more loving person. Changes that also made me a better, more responsible, and more productive employee.

In the world of recovery, dealing with the spiritual aspects of our disease isn't optional, it's mandatory. Because above all other things, sexual addiction is a disease of the heart and an intimacy disorder that, left undealt with, will simply leave them a shell of a person. Most recovering addicts quickly discover that seeking out a higher power is the only way to slay their personal demons. For me, I found solace in turning to the God of the Bible in what has evolved into a growing, personal relationship with God through Jesus Christ. Confessions have been made, sins have been forgiven, and a new life filled with eternal blessings and promises has given rise to a renewed sense of hope. This spiritual awakening has come about through my involvement in faith-based recovery groups that have been largely responsible for the good that now flows through my life into the hopes and dreams of others. That said, to embrace a willingness to offer employees the option of faith-based recovery in EAPs is not only evidence of a corporate culture that fully embraces respect for the individual, it is also good business.

The only question left to answer is, Will that company be yours, or someone else's? Will it be the dawning of a new day for you and your employees, or a return to the shell games of the past and business as usual? I think I know what my father would have said if he were still alive and faced with the same dilemma as a manager today. "We can't afford *not* to do everything possible to help our people— all of our people—thrive and grow. People are our greatest asset, and only when we begin to respect them and treat them that way can we ever really hope to reach our full potential as an organization."

There are a lot of things that have gone wrong in recent years with our free enterprise system, things that still need fixing, complex problems requiring the insight and energy of our brightest minds and bravest leaders. But until you've been to hell and back like me and many of my peers who have struggled to survive porn and sex addiction, you'll never know that beyond the shattered dreams of a life we once knew is the hope we all have for a second chance to shine. Humble and broken men and women who have lived most of their lives enslaved to a secret world of guilt and shame can and often do emerge from a successful recovery as far better people and much more capable employees and leaders. They will also be eager to take the message of healing and mercy and compassion that you've extended to them wherever they go in the hopes of sharing it with others, forever grateful for the freedom that came their way because someone believed in them, someone saw their true potential and took a chance.

Let's face it, it's easy to drive the bus with a bunch of well-ordered, self-managed people on board. No problems, no issues to deal with. It's what every manager secretly hopes for, and it makes for short days and stress-free living. But anyone with minimal management skills can do that. It's a whole other thing to take an average employee who's struggling with an addiction and help him tap into the true potential that lies hidden underneath the surface. To help him make the hard choices and face his fears and personal demons, only to emerge as a new person once he comes out on the other side of recovery. I've been fortunate enough to experience that several times, both in my own life and as I've shown others the way to freedom. And I can say without reservation that it's one of the most fulfilling, life-changing journeys you'll ever experience. And it can change the fortunes not only of one employee but of an entire organization.

After all, everyone loves a comeback story. They inspire us in ways that are hard to explain. Whether it's a business, a team, or an individual, we rally around people who once thought of themselves as losers but who turned into winners in the end. My hope in writing this book is that you, the reader, whatever your job might be and regardless of your station in life, will banish the notion that there are people unworthy or undeserving of someone's helping hand. People who think they are losers are winners just waiting to be discovered. They are waiting for the right person to come along who can see beyond their smoke screen of hurts and pains and insecurities. Someone bold enough to believe in them and brave enough to tell them so, to offer them a second chance when maybe no one else will.

The people in your organization who struggle in secret with sexual compulsivity and addiction are diamonds in the rough waiting to be smoothed and polished. In every case, there'll be some grinding and smoothing of the edges they'll have to endure as they undergo a much-needed transformation. But if you can respect them enough to believe in what they're capable of becoming, and if you can genuinely support those who are broken enough to want to get well, you just might discover that you've been sitting on a diamond mine of an organization for a very long time. When you find yourself in that place, as the agent of change and the beacon of hope for the hopeless, trust me when I tell you that your light will never burn brighter and your life will never be the same.

NOTES

Preface: Still Addicted to Sex

1. Betsy Morris, "Addicted to Sex: A Primal Problem Emerges from the Shadows in a New—and Dangerous—Corporate Environment," *Fortune*, May 10, 1999.

2. Andrew R. McIlvaine, "Internet Addiction: The Next Disability?" *Human Resource Executive Online*, http://www.hrexecutive.com/HRE/story.jsp?storyId=9942461 (accessed Sept 10, 2008).

3. Ogletree Deakins, "Employers Have Duty to Investigate Worker's Online Pornography Viewing," *Employment Law Information Network*, http://www.elinfonet.com/starticles/31/22/2 (accessed Sept 10, 2008).

4. "Knicks Lose Big in Sex Harassment Suit: Coach Isiah Thomas Guilty; Madison Square Garden Must Pay Former Exec $11.6M," *CBS News*, http://www.cbsnews.com/stories/2007/10/02/sports/main3318386.shtml (accessed Sept 10, 2008).

5. John Simons, "A Sex Scandal Is in the Mix at Sara Lee," *Fortune*, September 6, 2004.

6. Christopher Cornell, "FedEx Driver Wins Sex-Harassment Case," *Human Resource Executive Online*, http://www.hrexecutive.com/HRE/story.jsp?query=enforcing&storyId=4222585 (accessed Sept 10, 2008).

7. Dina Cappiello, "Government Officials Handling Oil Royalties Probed about Illicit Sex, Gifts," *San Jose Mercury News*, September 10, 2008.

8. Danny Hakim and William K. Rashbaum, "Spitzer Is Linked to Prostitution Ring," *New York Times*, March 10, 2008.

9. Julie Bloom, "Duchovny in Rehab," *New York Times*, August 29, 2008.

10. Michael Settle, "Lord Laidlaw Seeks Help for Sex Addiction after Lurid Revelations," *The Herald*, April 28, 2008.

11. Charles Babington and Jonathan Weisman, "Rep. Foley Quits in Page Scandal," *The Washington Post*, September 30, 2006.

12. Stephanie Armour, "Technology Makes Porn Easier to Access at Work," *USA Today*, October 17, 2007.

Introduction: Every Office's Dirty Secret

1. Stephanie Armour, "Technology Makes Porn Easier to Access at Work," *USA Today*, October 17, 2007.

2. Ibid.

Chapter 2: Using Porn @ Work

1. Dr. Drew Pinsky, *Dr. Drew Live*, Westwood One, May 16, 2008, interview with Michael Leahy.

Chapter 3: A Perfect Storm

1. "Sex on TV 4," a biennial study conducted by the Henry J. Kaiser Family Foundation, www.kff.org.

2. American Academy of Pediatrics, Committee on Public Education, "Media Violence," *Pediatrics* 108 no. 5 (Nov 5, 2001), http://aappolicy.aappublications.org/cgi/content/full/pediatrics;108/5/1222.

3. Lori O'Keefe, "Pediatricians Should 'Tune In' to Patients' Media Habits," American Academy of Pediatrics, *AAP News*, January 2001.

4. Rebecca Collins et al., "Watching Sex on Television Predicts Adolescent Initiation of Sexual Behavior," *Pediatrics* 114 no. 3 (2004): 280–89.

5. According to *The American Heritage Dictionary of the English Language: Fourth Edition*, 2000, definitions of pornography include: "1. Sexually explicit pictures, writing, or other material whose primary purpose is to cause sexual arousal. 2. The presentation or production of this material. 3. Lurid or sensational material."

6. Al Cooper, David L. Delmonico, and Ron Burg, "Cybersex Users, Abusers, and Compulsives: New Findings and Implications," in *Cybersex: The Dark Side of the Force*, ed. Al Cooper (Philadelphia: Brunner-Routledge, 2000), 6.

7. Suzanne Vranica, "Reinvent the Wheel in 2004—or Risk Being Flattened by It," *Wall Street Journal*, January 7, 2004.

8. Neil Malamuth and James Check, "The Effects of Aggressive Pornography on Beliefs in Rape Myths: Individual Differences," *Journal of Research in Personality* 19 (1985): 299–320. For related information see C. Everett Koop, "Report of the Surgeon General's Workshop on Pornography and Public Health," *American Psychologist* 42 (1987): 945.

Chapter 4: From Hobby to Health Hazard

1. Lauren Slater, "True Love: Scientists Say That the Brain Chemistry of Infatuation Is Akin to Mental Illness—Which Gives New Meaning to 'Madly in Love,'" *National Geographic*, February 2006, 32–50.

Chapter 5: Recognizing a Sex Addict @ Work

1. "The National Council on Sexual Addiction & Compulsivity estimated that 6%–8% of Americans are sex addicts, which is 16 million–21.5 million people." See Alvin Cooper, Dana E. Putnam, Lynn A. Planchon, and Sylvain C. Boies, "Online Sexual Compulsivity: Getting Tangled in the Net," *Sexual Addiction & Compulsivity* 6:2 (1999): 79–104.

2. Dr. Patrick Carnes, "Sex Addiction," SexHelp.com, http://www.sexhelp.com/addiction_ definitions.cfm.

3. Michael Herkov, Ph.D., "What Is Sexual Addiction?" PsychCentral.com, http://psychcentral.com/lib/2006/what-is-sexual-addiction/.

4. Mental Health Center, "Compulsive Sexual Behavior," MayoClinic.com, http://www.mayoclinic.com/health/compulsive-sexual-behavior/DS00144/.

5. Carnes, "Frequently Asked Questions," SexHelp.com, http://www.sexhelp.com/addiction_faq.cfm#how-many.

6. Alvin Cooper et al., "Online Sexual Compulsivity: Getting Tangled in the Net," *Sexual Addiction & Compulsivity* 6:2 (1999): 79–104.

7. Carnes, "Frequently Asked Questions," SexHelp.com, http://www.sexhelp.com/addiction_faq.cfm#multiple.

8. Ibid.

9. Carnes, "Frequently Asked Questions," SexHelp.com, http://www.sexhelp.com/addiction_faq.cfm#male-female.

10. Carnes, "Frequently Asked Questions," http://www.sexhelp.com/addiction_faq.cfm#behavior.

11. See Patrick Carnes, *Out of the Shadows: Understanding Sexual Addiction* (Center City, MN: Hazelden, 1992).

Chapter 6: The Graduates of Porn U: Today's Workforce

1. Carnes, "Frequently Asked Questions," SexHelp.com, http://www.sexhelp.com/addiction_faq.cfm#multiple.

Chapter 8: The "L" Word: What Keeps CEOs Up at Night

1. Andrew R. McIlvaine, "Internet Addiction: The Next Disability?" Human Resource Executive Online, http://www.hrexecutive.com/HRE/story.jsp?storyId=9942461 (accessed Sept 10, 2008).

2. Catherine Holahan, "Virtually Addicted," *BusinessWeek*, December 14, 2006.

3. Law offices of Littler Mendelson, newsletter, February 2006.

4. Adrienne Fox, "Caught in the Web," *Society for Human Resource Management*, http://www.shrm.org/hrmagazine/articles/1207/1207Fox2_cover.asp (accessed September 12, 2008).

APPENDIX A

Statistics on Pornography

Pornography Industry

Unless otherwise noted, the statistics below are found in Jerry Ropelato, "Internet Pornography Statistics" (www.toptenreviews. com), and are drawn from credible news and business sources.

- At $13.3 billion, the 2006 revenues of the sex and porn industry in the U.S. were bigger than the revenues of the NFL, NBA, and Major League Baseball combined.

- Worldwide sex industry sales for 2006 are reported to bc $97 billion, more revenue than Microsoft, Google, Amazon, eBay, Yahoo!, Apple, Netflix, and Earthlink combined. China is the largest consumer with $27.4 billion, South Korea is second at $25.7 billion, Japan is next at $20 billion, and the U.S. is fourth highest at $13.3 billion.

- Every second in the U.S., $3,075 is spent on pornography, 28,258 Internet users view pornography, and 372 Internet users type adult search terms into search engines.

- Pornographers currently release over 13,000 adult movies per year—more than 25 times the mainstream movie production.

Every 39 minutes a new pornographic video is being created in the United States.

- Approximately 20% of all Internet pornography involves children.
  – National Center for Missing & Exploited Children

- Comcast, the nation's largest cable company, pulled in $50 million from adult programming in 2003. The big hotel chains like Hilton, Marriott, Hyatt, Sheraton, and Holiday Inn all offer adult films on in-room pay-per-view television systems. Adult movies are purchased by a whopping 50% of their guests, accounting for nearly 70% of their in-room profits.
  – CBS News Special Report, November 2003

Pornography Use at Work

- Two-thirds of 474 human resources professionals said in a survey they've discovered pornography on employee computers. Nearly half of those, 43%, said they had found such material more than once.
  – Justin Bachman, AP Wire, October 23, 2003, regarding a study conducted by Business & Legal Reports, Old Saybrook, Connecticut

- 10% of U.S. adults admit to Internet sexual addiction, of which 28% are women.
  – Internet-Filter-Review.com

- More than 70% of men from ages 18 to 34 visit a pornographic site in a typical month.
  – comScore Media Metrix

- 70% of all online porn access occurs during the 9 to 5 workday.
  – Message Labs monthly report, March 2004

- A 2004 study of 350 companies in the U.S., the United Kingdom, and Australia found that one-third of workers admitted passing along porn at some time—and half of all workers said they'd been exposed to sexually explicit material by co-workers.
  – MSNBC, September 6, 2004, on a study conducted by Queen's University in Belfast

- 20% of men and 13% of women admitted to accessing pornography at work.

- The largest consumer of Internet pornography is the 35–49 age group.

- A study of university computer networks by Palisades Systems found searches for child pornography at 230 colleges nationwide. The research revealed that 42% of all searches on file-to-file sharing systems involved child or adult pornography. The study also found that 73% of movie searches were for pornography and 24% of image searches were for child pornography. Only 3% of the searches did not involve pornography or copyrighted materials.
  – Des Moines Register, April 1, 2003

- In May 2004 *BusinessWeek* printed the results of a comScore Networks survey in which 44% of U.S. workers with an Internet connection admitted to accessing an X-rated Web site at work in the month of March 2004, as compared to 40% of home users and 59% of university users.

- More than 30% of 1,500 surveyed companies have terminated employees for inappropriate use of the Internet, while only 37.5% of companies use filtering software.
  – Websense Incorporated and The Center for Internet Studies, 2000

- 70% of those who view pornography keep their habit a secret.
  - *MSNBC/Stanford/Duquesne Study in 2000*

- In 2003 the U.S. economy lost approximately 10 billion hours in productive work time. These hours amounted to an estimated $250 billion dollars in lost wage expenses paid to employees who chose to surf the Internet rather than work.

  - *Estimated by Internet Policy Consulting LLC, based on data from Computerworld, Nielsen/Net Ratings, comScore Media Metrix, UCLA, and their own estimates*

- Half of the Fortune 500 companies have dealt with at least one incident related to computer porn over a 12-month period. Offenders were fired in 44% of the incidents and disciplined in a further 41%.
  - *Computerworld, Vol. 11, Issue 17, July 14, 2005*

- Of 61 million unique U.S. visitors logged into pornographic Web sites in March of 2006, every fifth visitor was from an office workstation.
  - *comScore Media Metrix statistic, cited in "Pornography in the Workplace," SavannahNow.com, April 23, 2006*

- Nearly one-third of U.S. Fortune 500 companies have had sexual harassment cases filed against them by employees objecting to their colleagues' Internet viewing habits.
  - *"Avoid the Web of Deceit, Porn and Litigation," TimesOnline.co.uk/tol/news, September 5, 2005*

- In 2003 employees at the U.K. Dept of Work and Pensions downloaded some two million pages of pornographic content. Of these two million, some 1800 contained child pornography.
  - *"Workplace Porn, Alive and Well," Friday in Focus UK article*

The Impact of Pornography

- About 4 in every 10 U.S. adolescents age 10 to 17 report they've seen pornography while on the Internet, two-thirds of them saying it was uninvited, according to a 2007 study by the University of New Hampshire.

- 51% of U.S. adults surveyed believe that pornography raises men's expectations of how women should look and changes men's expectations of how women should behave. 40% of adults surveyed believe that pornography harms relationships between men and women.
  – Harris Poll, "No Consensus among American Public on the Effects of Pornography on Adults or Children or What Government Should Do About It," October 7, 2005

- 1 out of every 6 women grapples with addiction to pornography.
  – "Internet Pornography and Loneliness: An Association?" Vincent Cyrus Yoder, Thomas B. Virden III, and Kiran Amin, Sexual Addiction & Compulsivity, *Volume 12.1, 2005*

- At a 2003 meeting of the American Academy of Matrimonial Lawyers, two-thirds of the 350 divorce lawyers who attended said the Internet played a significant role in the divorces in the past year, with excessive interest in online porn contributing to more than half such cases. Pornography had an almost nonexistent role in divorce just seven or eight years prior.
  – Divorcewizards.com

- According to the report on Commercial Sexual Exploitation of Children in the U.S., 200,000 to 300,000 children are victims of commercial sexual exploitation in this country alone.
  – CSEC Report, "Overview of the CSEC in the United States"

APPENDIX B

The Sexual Addiction Screening Test
Developed by Dr. Patrick Carnes, founder, Sexhelp.com

The Sexual Addiction Screening Test (SAST) was developed by Dr. Patrick Carnes and has become one of several diagnostic tools commonly used to help determine to what degree a person's sexual behaviors might have become compulsive or addictive.

The core test consists of twenty-five yes/no questions, listed below. To take the test online and/or view composite test results, go to the Sex Survey page on our Web site at www.pornatworkthebook-.com. There you'll find a confidential online version of this SAST.

While taking the test, keep track of how many "yes" responses you have to the 25 core questions. That will be your score. At the end of the test, you'll find a general assessment of what your score might mean with regard to your overall sexual compulsivity and addictive tendencies. This test is in no way meant to provide a final or conclusive determination; it is just an early diagnostic tool.

To read more about how over 25,000 college and university students responded to this sex survey, please see my latest book, *Porn University: What College Students Are Really Saying about Sex on Campus.*

For the next 25 questions, keep a running tally of how many questions you answer "yes" to.

1. Were you sexually abused as a child or adolescent?

2. Do you regularly read romance novels or sexually explicit magazines, or regularly visit sexually explicit Web sites or chat rooms?

3. Have you stayed in romantic relationships after they become emotionally or physically abusive?

4. Do you often find yourself preoccupied with sexual thoughts or romantic daydreams?

5. Do you feel that your sexual behavior is not normal?

6. Does your spouse (or significant other[s]) ever worry or complain about your sexual behavior?

7. Do you have trouble stopping your sexual behavior when you know it is inappropriate?

8. Do you ever feel bad about your sexual behavior?

9. Has your sexual behavior ever created problems for you and your family or friends?

10. Have you ever sought help for sexual behavior you did not like?

11. Have you ever worried about people finding out about your sexual activities?

12. Has anyone been hurt emotionally because of your sexual behavior?

13. Have you ever participated in sexual activity in exchange for money or gifts?

14. Do you have times when you act out sexually followed by periods of celibacy (no sex at all)?

15. Have you made efforts to quit a type of sexual activity and failed?

16. Do you hide some of your sexual behavior from others?

17. Do you find yourself having multiple romantic relationships at the same time?

18. Have you ever felt degraded by your sexual behavior?

19. Has sex or romantic fantasies been a way for you to escape your problems?

20. When you have sex, do you feel depressed afterward?

21. Do you regularly engage in sadomasochistic behavior (S&M, i.e., sex with whips, leather, spanking, pain, etc.)?

22. Has your sexual activity interfered with your family life?

23. Have you been sexual with minors?

24. Do you feel controlled by your sexual desire or fantasies of romance?

25. Do you ever think your sexual desire is stronger than you are?

SAST Risk Assessment

Your score—the total number of "yes" responses you had in the last 25 questions of the Sexual Addiction Screening Test (SAST)—determines which one of three risk behavior groups described below that you fall into: low risk, at risk, or high risk.

Low Risk (0–8)

You may or may not have a problem with sexually compulsive behavior. However, if your sexual behavior is causing you problems in your life, we encourage you to confide in a trusted friend for support and personal accountability and consider seeking the help of a professional counselor or health care specialist with experience in this area who can conduct further assessment.

At Risk (9–18)

You are "at-risk" for your sexual behavior to interfere with significant areas of your life. If you are concerned about your sexual behavior and have noticed consequences as a result, you should confide in a trusted friend for accountability and seek out the help of a professional counselor or health care specialist with experience in this area who can conduct a further assessment.

High Risk (19–25)

You are in the highest risk group for your sexual behavior to interfere with and jeopardize important areas of your life (social, occupational, educational, etc.). It is essential that you share this in confidence with a trusted friend or confidant who is willing and able to keep this confidential yet hold you accountable for your actions. It is also strongly recommended that you discuss your compulsive and addictive sexual behavior with a professional counselor or health care specialist experienced in this area of work to further assess your condition. Also see our Hope & Help page at www.pornnationthebook.com for a list of resources and tools for recovery.

APPENDIX C

Recommended Reading and Other Resources for Recovery

The books, recovery groups, and services listed below are intended to provide the reader with more information or a starting point from which they can begin their recovery. This list is a recommended sampling of the many resources that are available.

Recommended Reading

In addition to the books and articles cited in the endnotes, the following is a recommended reading list:

The White Book of Sexaholics Anonymous, SA Literature, 1989

False Intimacy: Understanding the Struggle of Sexual Addiction, Dr. Harry Schaumburg, NavPress, 1997

The Purity Principle, Randy Alcorn, Multnomah, 2003

Contrary to Love: Helping the Sexual Addict, Dr. Patrick Carnes, Hazelden, 1994

Don't Call It Love: Recovery from Sexual Addiction, Dr. Patrick Carnes, Bantam, 1991

Waking the Dead: The Glory of a Heart Fully Alive, John Eldredge, Thomas Nelson, 2003

Sex God: Exploring the Endless Connections between Sexuality and Spirituality, Rob Bell, Zondervan, 2007

Flesh: An Unbreakable Habit of Purity in a Pornographic World: Men's Edition, Rick James, WSN Press, 2004

Fantasy: An Insatiable Desire for a Satisfying Love: Women's Edition, Betty Blake Churchill with Rick James, Cru Press, 2005

Recovery Groups, Software, and Other Resources

Sexual Addiction Twelve-Step Groups

Sexaholics Anonymous (SA)
PO Box 3565
Brentwood, TN 37024
Web site: www.sa.org
Email: saico@sa.org
Phone: 615-370-6062

Sex Addicts Anonymous (SAA)
ISO of SAA
PO Box 70949
Houston, TX 77270
Web site: www.saa-recovery.org
Email: info@saa-recovery.org
Phone: 800-477-8191 or 713-869-4902

Sex and Love Addicts Anonymous (SLAA)
Fellowship-Wide Services
1550 NE Loop 410, Ste 118
San Antonio, TX 78209
Web site: www.slaafws.org
Email: generalinfo@slaafws.org
Phone: 210-828-7900

Faith-based Recovery Groups

Celebrate Recovery
25422 Trabuco Rd. #105-151
Lake Forest, CA 92630
Web site: www.celebraterecovery.com
Email: info@celebraterecovery.com
Phone: 949-581-0548

Bethesda Workshops
3710 Franklin Rd.
Nashville, TN 37204
Web site: www.bethesdaworkshops.org
Email: mferree@bethesdaworkshops.org
Phone: 866-464-4325 or 615-467-5610

L.I.F.E. Ministries / LIFE Groups
PO Box 952317
Lake Mary, FL 32795
Web site: www.freedomeveryday.org
Email: info@freedomeveryday.org
Phone: 866-408-LIFE

Pure Online

660 Preston Forest Center
Dallas, TX 75230
Web site: www.pureonline.com
Email: support@pureonline.com
Phone: 214-580-2000

Internet Filtering and Accountability Tools

Net Nanny

2369 West Orton Circle
Salt Lake City, UT 84119
Web site: www.netnanny.com
Email: info@contentwatch.com
Phone: 800-485-4008 or 801-977-7777

Covenant Eyes

1525 West King St.
Owosso, MI 48867
Web site: www.covenanteyes.com
Email: info@covenanteyes.com
Phone: 877-479-1119

Bsafe Online

PO Box 1819
Bristol, TN 37621
Web site: www.bsafehome.com
Phone: 850-362-4310

ACKNOWLEDGMENTS

This is a book that I have wanted to write for a very long time, so there are a lot of people to thank whose support, insights, and contributions have helped to make this project a reality.

Instead of saving her acknowledgement for last as I've had a habit of doing in past books, I really need to first thank my wonderful bride, Christine, for her ever-present encouragement, including those hundreds of text messages she would send me asking "How's the writing going?" or more like "Have you started writing yet today?" Chrissy, you know me oh so well. Thank you for your endless patience. I love you.

I dedicated this book to my father who taught me many of my first lessons in life about work and family and life and love. But I would be remiss in not mentioning and thanking my mother, Patricia, aka Mona, the other half of this dynamic duo. Mom, I know how much this book means to you, but you were just as responsible for my being able to write it as Dad was. Thanks for sticking it out through fifty-three years of marriage and showing all of us what committed love and a true marriage partnership really look like.

To Andy, Randall, Lori, and the whole team at Moody Publishing, for believing in the importance of this writing project just as much as I do. Thank you for your continued commitment to the BraveHearts mission and to me personally. You are a wonderful partner and I look forward to many more years of writing and working together.

To David and Rebekah and both Elizabeths at Credo Communications, I love working with you guys. You're the best literary agent firm ever and you continue to keep me in awe of your commitment to excellence. Especially to Elizabeth Jones, thank you for convincing God to hold off on bringing your new baby Titus into this world until after the bulk of your editing of the final manuscript was done. I'm thankful that you both are healthy and well and can't believe that you actually edited two book manuscripts for me while you were in your last trimester. You're amazing.

Thanks also to Dr. Patrick Carnes and his staff for your pioneering effort and years of dedicated service in the area of sexual compulsivity and addiction research and recovery. You have no idea how important your work has been to the millions of us who have struggled with this disorder to one degree or another throughout our lives.

To the many wonderful people I've had the opportunity to work with and for over the years, especially my brother Joe and Doug, Nick, Tony and Rick, Regi and Tut, Kevin and Blake, Boyd and Fran, and Don and Carey. You've all taught me so very much, and I remain forever indebted to your kindness and compassion in supporting what I do today.

ABOUT *the* AUTHOR

Michael Leahy is a recovering sex addict and the founder and executive director of BraveHearts, an organization dedicated to increasing the public's awareness of the hidden dangers and long-term consequences of pornography consumption. Before launching BraveHearts in 2002, Michael was a sales executive in the computer industry and worked for blue-chip corporations like IBM, Unisys, and NEC, as well as a number of midsized and small businesses. Michael is the father of two boys, Chris (22) and Andrew (14). His first marriage ended in divorce in 1998 after his thirty-year relationship with pornography escalated into a self-destructive affair that exposed a lifelong struggle with sexual compulsivity and addiction.

Now ten years into recovery, Michael has appeared in numerous national television broadcasts and print media, including *20/20*, *The View*, and *USA Today* as an expert on the subjects of pornography, sexual addiction, and the impact sex in media is having on our society. He's shared his compelling story and expertise in churches, at conferences, and with over 100,000 students on more than 150 college campuses worldwide in his critically acclaimed, multimedia-intensive live-speaker presentation called "Porn Nation: The Naked Truth." Michael is remarried and currently resides with his wife, Christine, in the Washington, D.C. area.

PORN NATION

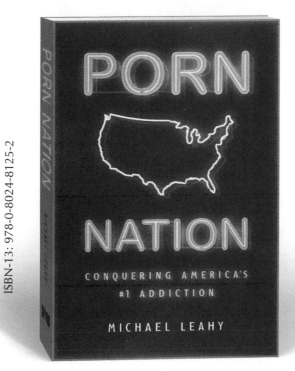

Pornography and sex-related sites make up nearly 60 percent of daily web traffic. For some of us, it's going on in our very own basements or in the den after the family goes to bed. Over twenty million Americans spend a good deal of their waking hours looking at pornography. And they won't stop, because they can't stop. At least not on their own. They are addicted. But it's also the story of the rest of us. It's the story of America – our porn nation. How is it affecting us? How is it changing the way we see ourselves and others? And what can be done about it?

NORTHFIELD
PUBLISHING

1-800-678-8812 • MOODYPUBLISHERS.COM

PORN UNIVERSITY

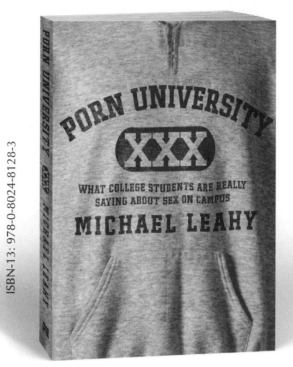

ISBN-13: 978-0-8024-8128-3

Porn University reveals the startling results of a brand-new study on the sexual attitudes, beliefs, and behaviors of more than 25,000 college and university students on more than 100 campuses all over America. The revealing results offer a closer look at the shifting sexual trends and histories of the next generation of leaders in America. Included is commentary and analysis from the author and other experts in this field on key findings and discoveries, as well as predictions of where the sexual trends of tomorrow might be headed. Don't be discouraged. There is hope!

NORTHFIELD
PUBLISHING

1-800-678-8812 • MOODYPUBLISHERS.COM